Richard Garnett

Relics of Shelley

Richard Garnett

Relics of Shelley

ISBN/EAN: 9783743306813

Manufactured in Europe, USA, Canada, Australia, Japa

Cover: Foto ©ninafisch / pixelio.de

Manufactured and distributed by brebook publishing software (www.brebook.com)

Richard Garnett

Relics of Shelley

RELICS OF SHELLEY.

EDITED BY

RICHARD GARNETT.

"Sing again, with your dear voice revealing
A tone
Of some world far from ours,
Where music and moonlight and feeling
Are one."

LONDON:
EDWARD MOXON & CO., DOVER STREET.
1862.

PREFACE.

In her preface to Shelley's *Posthumous Poems* (1824), Mrs. Shelley observes :—

"I do not know whether the critics will reprehend the insertion of some of the most imperfect among these; but I frankly own, that I have been more actuated by the fear lest any monument of his genius should escape me, than the wish of presenting nothing but what was complete to the fastidious reader. I feel secure that the lovers of Shelley's Poetry (who know how more than any other poet of the present day, every line and word he wrote is instinct with peculiar beauty) will pardon and thank me. I consecrate this Volume to them."

No one, assuredly, ever reprehended the publication of any portion of the Posthumous Poems; but an apology which, prefixed to these, must appear the excess of modesty, may not be out of place when indulgence is solicited for far more incomplete remains of a writer who certainly never contemplated, and probably would not have sanctioned, their publication. It can only be pleaded that the imperfection of these fragments, compared with those given to the world in 1824, is more than counterbalanced by the corresponding advance of the author's fame, and the augmented interest felt in his history and writings. There are thousands to whom hardly any unpublished production of Shelley's could be unacceptable, and the gratification of a liberal and affectionate curiosity might have excused the publication even of a more imperfect work. If, however, these pages add nothing to the list of Shelley's masterpieces, they will at all events contain nothing in any way disadvantageous to his reputation, and, at least with readers who bring the capacity for enjoyment with them, will even be found to extend it in several respects.

The sublimity of some parts of the "Prologue to Hellas;" the exquisite fancifulness of "Una Favola;" and "The Magic Plant;" the sweetness of the "Lines in the Bay of Lerici;" the vividness of some of the briefer expressions of feeling, require no expositor, and no panegyrist. The value of the rest is perhaps chiefly psychological; they extend our knowledge and intensify our conception of the writer's character. We seem to attain to a more intimate acquaintance with a great spirit when listening to its first unstudied utterances, than by receiving these elaborated for the press—or, perhaps, something in their place which the author wishes *had* been his first thought. Such is, indeed, rarely the case with Shelley, whose sincerity is above all suspicion, and whose ceaseless revision, while it introduced the most extensive modifications into the form of his writings, rarely affected the substance, or effaced the delicate bloom of the original conception. The shortcomings of the pieces now made public, afford, indeed, the best testimony of the diligence with which he elaborated his works, for there is hardly one of his most admired productions of which the original draft is not equally imperfect; and nothing but corresponding labour was wanting to have advanced almost any of these to corresponding excellence. The unity of spirit which pervades these equally with his more finished works, must speak for his sincerity, and the sentiments to which they give expression will prove how exclusively his lonely musings were devoted to exalted or pathetic themes. Few have borne so severe a scrutiny. Almost every verse he ever pencilled down, has now become the property of the public,* and any reader, with the reservation before made, may say in his own words:—

> "I am as a spirit who has dwelt
> Within his heart of hearts, and I have felt
> His feelings, and have thought his thoughts, and known
> The inmost converse of his soul."

---

* The principal exception consists in the numerous MS. additions to "Charles I." and "Mazenghi," the publication of which would have involved the reproduction of much that had already been printed.

Publication having been determined upon, fairness to the present possessors of Shelley's writings evidently demanded that it should at first take place in a separate volume, previously to the incorporation of these fragments with their author's collected works.

Many of them had been already collected by Mrs. Shelley, whose transcript has materially facilitated the Editor's labours. Many others, and among these the most important, are the fruit of a recent examination of Shelley's MS. books. They appear to have been hitherto overlooked, for the reason that must also serve as an excuse for the imperfect manner in which they are even now presented to the public—the extremely confused state of these books, and the equal difficulty of deciphering and of connecting their contents. Being written in great haste, and frequently with the pencil, the handwriting is often indistinct of itself, and rendered far more so by erasures and interlineations *ad infinitum*. Shelley appears to have composed with the pen in his hand, and to have corrected as fast as he wrote; hence a page full of writing frequently yields only two or three available lines, which must be painfully disentangled from a chaos of obliterations.* Much that at first sight wears the appearance of novelty, proves on inspection to be merely a variation of something already published; and sometimes the case is reversed, as in the "Prologue to Hellas," so buried in the MS. of that drama (which has in itself on the average ten lines effaced for one retained), as to be only discoverable or separable upon very close scrutiny. The connection, moreover, of the component parts of the same piece is frequently difficult to ascertain, scattered as these

---

* Mr. Trelawny says of the original MS. draft of "Lines to a Lady with a Guitar:"—"It was a frightful scrawl; words smeared out with his finger, and one upon the other, over and over in tiers, and all run together in most admired disorder; it might have been taken for a sketch of a marsh, overgrown with bulrushes, and the blots for wild ducks." ("Recollections," p. 74.) The MS. thus graphically described is not forthcoming; but the description is sufficiently applicable to many others. When Shelley wrote for the printer, his handwriting was singularly neat and beautiful.

are over several MS. books, and interspersed with a great variety of other matter. It cannot, therefore, be expected that the text of these fragments should be in all respects correct; here the right reading may be doubtful, there the right order; here conjecture has filled up a chasm, there, perhaps, inadvertence or misapprehension has created another. It may, however, be hoped that the sum of all errors is not very great, and if some new mistakes have been committed, many old ones have been rectified, as will appear in its place.

Of the other contents of this Volume it is not necessary to say much. It has been earnestly endeavoured to avoid anything approaching to book-making;—an object which will not have been attained should anything have been printed wholly uninteresting to those who are interested in Shelley. Of such of its contents as do not immediately emanate from his pen, perhaps none will be so acceptable as the few letters from Mrs. Shelley, which must confirm the opinion, prevalent since the publication of the "Memorials," that the compositions published in her lifetime afford but an inadequate conception of the intense sensibility and mental vigour of this extraordinary woman.

March, 1862.

CONTENTS.

	PAGE
PROLOGUE TO HELLAS	3
THE MAGIC PLANT	14
ORPHEUS	20
SCENE FROM TASSO	26
FIORDISPINA	28
TO HIS GENIUS	34
LOVE, HOPE, DESIRE, AND FEAR	40
LINES	43
LINES WRITTEN IN THE BAY OF LERICI	45
FRAGMENTS OF THE ADONAIS	48
TRANSLATION OF THE FIRST CANZONE OF DANTE'S CONVITO	53
MATILDA GATHERING FLOWERS	56
TRANSLATION OF HOMER'S HYMN TO VENUS	59
UNA FAVOLA	62

CONTENTS.

	PAGE
A FABLE [TRANSLATION]	67
MISCELLANEOUS FRAGMENTS	74
ON THE TEXT OF SHELLEY'S POEMS	92
LETTERS TO LEIGH HUNT	101
SHELLEY, HARRIET SHELLEY, AND MR. T. L. PEACOCK	145
LINES AT BOSCOMBE	175
APPENDIX	183

POEMS,
ETC.

PROLOGUE TO HELLAS.

[Mrs. Shelley informs us, in her note on the "Prometheus Unbound," that at the time of her husband's arrival in Italy, he meditated the production of three dramas. One of these was the "Prometheus" itself; the second, a drama on the subject of Tasso's madness; the third one founded on the Book of Job; "of which," she adds, "he never abandoned the idea." That this was the case will be apparent from the following newly-discovered fragment, which may have been, as I have on the whole preferred to describe it, an unfinished prologue to "Hellas," or perhaps the original sketch of that work, discarded for the existing more dramatic, but less ambitious version, for which the "Persae" of Æschylus evidently supplied the model. It is written in the same book as the original MS. of "Hellas," and so blended with this as to be only separable after very minute examination. Few even of Shelley's rough drafts have proved more difficult to decipher or connect; numerous chasms will be observed, which, with every diligence, it has proved impossible to fill up; the correct reading of many printed lines is far from certain; and the imperfection of some passages is such as to have occasioned their entire omission. Nevertheless, I am confident that the unpolished and mutilated remnant will be accepted as a worthy emanation of one of Shelley's sublimest moods, and a noble earnest of what he might have accomplished could he have executed his original design of founding a drama on the Book of Job. Weak health, variable spirits, above all, the absence of encouragement, must be enumerated as chief among the causes which have deprived our literature of so magnificent a work.]

HERALD OF ETERNITY.

It is the day when all the sons of God
Wait in the roofless senate-house, whose floor
Is Chaos, and the immovable abyss
Frozen by His steadfast word to hyaline
  * * * * *
The shadow of God, and delegate
Of that before whose breath the universe
Is as a print of dew.
      Hierarchs and kings
Who from your thrones pinnacled on the past
Sway the reluctant present, ye who sit
Pavilioned on the radiance or the gloom
Of mortal thought, which like an exhalation
Steaming from earth, conceals the   of heaven
Which gave it birth,   assemble here
Before your Father's throne; the swift decree
Yet hovers, and the fiery incarnation
Is yet withheld, clothed in which it shall
            annul
The fairest of those wandering isles that gem
The sapphire space of interstellar air,
That green and azure sphere, that earth inwrapt
Less in the beauty of its tender light
Than in an atmosphere of living spirit

Which interpenetrating all the
                 it rolls from realm to realm
And age to age, and in its ebb and flow
Impels the generations
To their appointed place,
Whilst the high Arbiter
Beholds the strife, and at the appointed time
Sends his decrees veiled in eternal

Within the circuit of this pendant orb
There lies an antique region, on which fell
The dews of thought in the world's golden dawn
Earliest and most benign, and from it sprung
Temples and cities and immortal forms
And harmonies of wisdom and of song,
And thoughts, and deeds worthy of thoughts so fair.
And when the sun of its dominion failed,
And when the winter of its glory came,
The winds that stript it bare blew on and swept
That dew into the utmost wildernesses
In wandering clouds of sunny rain that thawed
The unmaternal bosom of the North.
Haste, sons of God,   for ye beheld,
Reluctant, or consenting, or astonished,
The stern decrees go forth, which heaped on Greece
Ruin and degradation and despair.
A fourth now waits: assemble, sons of God,

To speed or to prevent or to suspend,
If, as ye dream, such power be not withheld,
The unaccomplished destiny.

   *   *   *   *   *

CHORUS.

The curtain of the Universe
  Is rent and shattered,
The splendour-wingèd worlds disperse
  Like wild doves scattered.

Space is roofless and bare,
And in the midst a cloudy shrine,
  Dark amid thrones of light.
In the blue glow of hyaline
Golden worlds revolve and shine
  In   flight
  From every point of the Infinite,
  Like a thousand dawns on a single night
The splendours rise and spread;
And through thunder and darkness dread
Light and music are radiated,
And in their pavilioned chariots led
By living wings high overhead
  The giant Powers move,
Gloomy or bright as the thrones they fill.

* * * * *
 A chaos of light and motion
  Upon that glassy ocean.
* * * * *
 The senate of the Gods is met,
 Each in his rank and station set;
 There is silence in the spaces—
 Lo! Satan, Christ, and Mahomet
 Start from their places!
* * * * *

CHRIST.

   Almighty Father!
Low-kneeling at the feet of Destiny
* * * * *
There are two fountains in which spirits weep
When mortals err, Discord and Slavery named,
And with their bitter dew two Destinies
Filled each their irrevocable urns; the third,
Fiercest and mightiest, mingled both, and added
Chaos and Death, and slow Oblivion's lymph,
And hate and terror, and the poisoned rain
* * * * *
The Aurora of the nations. By this brow
Whose pores wept tears of blood, by these wide
  wounds,
By this imperial crown of agony,

By infamy and solitude and death,
For this I underwent, and by the pain
Of pity for those who would   for me
The unremembered joy of a revenge,
For this I felt—by Plato's sacred light,
Of which my spirit was a burning morrow—
By Greece and all she cannot cease to be,
Her quenchless words, sparks of immortal truth,
Stars of all night—her harmonies and forms,
Echoes and shadows of what Love adores
In thee, I do compel thee, send forth Fate,
Thy irrevocable child : let her descend
A seraph-wingèd victory [arrayed]
In tempest of the omnipotence of God
Which sweeps through all things.

From hollow leagues, from Tyranny which arms
Adverse miscreeds and emulous anarchies
To stamp, as on a wingèd serpent's seed,
Upon the name of Freedom ; from the storm
Of faction, which like earthquake shakes and sickens
The solid heart of enterprise ; from all
By which the holiest dreams of highest spirits
Are stars beneath the dawn

                        She shall arise
Victorious as the world arose from Chaos !

And as the Heavens and the Earth arrayed
Their presence in the beauty and the light
Of thy first smile, O Father, as they gather
The spirit of thy love which paves for them
Their path o'er the abyss, till every sphere
Shall be one living Spirit, so shall Greece—

SATAN.

Be as all things beneath the empyrean,
Mine! Art thou eyeless like old Destiny,
Thou mockery-king, crowned with a wreath of thorns?
Whose sceptre is a reed, the broken reed
Which pierces thee! whose throne a chair of scorn;
For seest thou not beneath this crystal floor
The innumerable worlds of golden light
Which are my empire, and the least of them
     which thou would'st redeem from me?
Know'st thou not them my portion?
Or wouldst rekindle the   strife
Which our great Father then did arbitrate
When he assigned to his competing sons
Each his apportioned realm?
      Thou Destiny,
Thou who art mailed in the omnipotence
Of Him who sends thee forth, whate'er thy task,
Speed, spare not to accomplish, and be mine
Thy trophies, whether Greece again become

The fountain in the desert whence the earth
Shall drink of freedom, which shall give it strength
To suffer, or a gulph of hollow death
To swallow all delight, all life, all hope.
Go, thou Vicegerent of my will, no less
Than of the Father's; but lest thou shouldst faint,
The wingèd hounds, Famine and Pestilence,
Shall wait on thee, the hundred-forkèd snake,
Insatiate Superstition, still shall
The earth behind thy steps, and War shall hover
Above, and Fraud shall gape below, and Change
Shall flit before thee on her dragon wings,
Convulsing and consuming, and I add
Three vials of the tears which demons weep
When virtuous spirits through the gate of Death
Pass triumphing over the thorns of life,
Sceptres and crowns, mitres and swords and snares,
Trampling in scorn, like Him and Socrates.
The first is Anarchy; when Power and Pleasure,
Glory and science and security,
On Freedom hang like fruit on the green tree,
Then pour it forth, and men shall gather ashes.
The second Tyranny—

CHRIST.

Obdurate spirit!
Thou seest but the Past in the To-come.

Pride is thy error and thy punishment.
Boast not thine empire, dream not that thy worlds
Are more than furnace-sparks or rainbow-drops
Before the Power that wields and kindles them.
True greatness asks not space, true excellence
Lives in the Spirit of all things that live,
Which lends it to the worlds thou callest thine.

* * * * *

MAHOMET.

* * * * *

Haste thou and fill the waning crescent
With beams as keen as those which pierced the shadow
Of Christian night rolled back upon the West
When the orient moon of Islam rode in triumph
From Tmolus to the Acroceraunian snow.

* * * * *

Wake, thou Word
Of God, and from the throne of Destiny
Even to the utmost limit of thy way
May Triumph

* * * * *

Be thou a curse on them whose creed
Divides and multiplies the most high God.

1821.

[The following fragments appear to have been originally written for "Hellas."]

> Fairest of the Destinies,
> Disarray thy dazzling eyes:
> Keener far their lightnings are
> Than the wingèd [bolts] thou bearest,
> > And the smile thou wearest
> > Wraps thee as a star
> > Is wrapt in light.

Could Arethuse to her forsaken urn
From Alpheus and the bitter Doris run,
Or could the morning shafts of purest light
Again into the quivers of the Sun
Be gathered—could one thought from its wild flight
Return into the temple of the brain
> Without a change, without a stain,—
> Could aught that is, ever again
> Be what it once has ceased to be,
> > Greece might again be free!

> A star has fallen upon the earth
> > 'Mid the benighted nations,
> A quenchless atom of immortal light,
> > A living spark of Night,
> A cresset shaken from the constellations.

Swifter than the thunder fell
To the heart of Earth, the well
Where its pulses flow and beat,
And unextinct in that cold source
Burns, and on   course
Guides the sphere which is its prison,
Like an angelic spirit pent
In a form of mortal birth,
Till, as a spirit half arisen
Shatters its charnel, it has rent,
In the rapture of its mirth,
The thin and painted garment of the Earth,
   Ruining its chaos—a fierce breath
Consuming all its forms of living death.

THE MAGIC PLANT.

[THE readers of Shelley's writings will remember, among the poems of 1822, a fragment of a romantic drama which, Mrs. Shelley tells us, was "undertaken for the amusement of the individuals who composed our intimate society, but left unfinished." A close scrutiny, however, of one of Shelley's numerous MS. books has revealed the existence of much more of this piece than has hitherto been suspected to exist. By far the larger portion of this, forming an episode complete in itself, is here made public, under the title of "The Magic Plant." To have published the remainder would have involved the necessity of reproducing the whole of what had previously been printed: it has been thought preferable to await the appearance of a new edition of Shelley's complete works.

The little drama of which this charming sport of fancy forms a portion was written at Pisa, during the late winter or early spring of 1822. The episode of "The Magic Plant" was obviously suggested by the pleasure Shelley received from the plants grown in-doors in his Pisan dwelling, which, he says, in a letter written in January, 1822, "turn the sunny winter into spring." See also the poem of "The Zucca," composed about the same time.]

LADY.

METHOUGHT a star came down from heaven,
And rested 'mid the plants of India,
Which I had given a shelter from the frost

Within my chamber. There the meteor lay,
Panting forth light among the leaves and flowers,
As if it lived, and was outworn with speed;
Or that it loved, and passion made the pulse
Of its bright life throb like an anxious heart,
Till it diffused itself, and all the chamber
And walls seemed melted into emerald fire
That burned not; in the midst of which appeared
A spirit like a child, and laughed aloud
A thrilling peal of such sweet merriment
As made the blood tingle in my warm feet:
Then bent over a vase, and murmuring
Low, unintelligible melodies,
Placed something in the mould like melon-seeds,
And slowly faded, and in place of it
A soft hand issued from the veil of fire,
Holding a cup like a magnolia flower,
And poured upon the earth within the vase
The element with which it overflowed,
Brighter than morning light, and purer than
The water of the springs of Himalah.

YOUTH.

You waked not?

LADY.

Not until my dream became
Like a child's legend on the tideless sand,

Which the first foam erases half, and half
Leaves legible. At length I rose, and went,
Visiting my flowers from pot to pot, and thought
To set new cuttings in the empty urns,
And when I came to that beside the lattice,
I saw two little dark-green leaves
Lifting the light mould at their birth, and then
I half-remembered my forgotten dream.
And day by day, green as a gourd in June,
The plant grew fresh and thick, yet no one knew
What plant it was ; its stem and tendrils seemed
Like emerald snakes, mottled and diamonded
With azure mail and streaks of woven silver ;
And all the sheaths that folded the dark buds
Rose like the crest of cobra-di-capel,
Until the golden eye of the bright flower
Through the dark lashes of those veined lids,
  disencumbered of their silent sleep,
Gazed like a star into the morning light.
Its leaves were delicate, you almost saw
The pulses
With which the purple velvet flower was fed
To overflow, and like a poet's heart
Changing bright fancy to sweet sentiment,
Changed half the light to fragrance. It soon fell,
And to a green and dewy embryo-fruit
Left all its treasured beauty. Day by day

I nursed the plant, and on the double flute
Played to it on the sunny winter days
Soft melodies, as sweet as April rain
On silent leaves, and sang those words in which
Passion makes Echo taunt the sleeping strings;
And I would send tales of forgotten love
Late into the lone night, and sing wild songs
Of maids deserted in the olden time,
And weep like a soft cloud in April's bosom
Upon the sleeping eyelids of the plant,
So that perhaps it dreamed that Spring was come,
And crept abroad into the moonlight air,
And loosened all its limbs, as, noon by noon,
The sun averted less his oblique beam.

YOUTH.

And the plant died not in the frost?

LADY.

It grew;
And went out of the lattice which I left
Half open for it, trailing its quaint spires
Along the garden and across the lawn,
And down the slope of moss and through the tufts
Of wild-flower roots, and stumps of trees o'ergrown
With simple lichens, and old hoary stones,
On to the margin of the glassy pool,

Even to a nook of unblown violets
And lilies-of-the-valley yet unborn,
Under a pine with ivy overgrown.
And there its fruit lay like a sleeping lizard
Under the shadows; but when Spring indeed
Came to unswathe her infants, and the lilies
Peeped from their bright green masks to wonder at
This shape of Autumn couched in their recess,
Then it dilated, and it grew until
One half lay floating on the fountain wave,
Whose pulse, elapsed in unlike sympathies,
Kept time
Among the snowy water-lily buds.
Its shape was such as summer melody
Of the south wind in spicy vales might give
To some light cloud bound from the golden dawn
To fairy isles of evening, and it seemed
In hue and form that it had been a mirror
Of all the hues and forms around it and
Upon it pictured by the sunny beams
Which, from the bright vibrations of the pool,
Were thrown upon the rafters and the roof
Of boughs and leaves, and on the pillared stems
Of the dark sylvan temple, and reflections
Of every infant flower and star of moss
And veined leaf in the azure odorous air.
And thus it lay in the Elysian calm

Of its own beauty, floating on the line
Which, like a film in purest space, divided
The heaven beneath the water from the heaven
Above the clouds; and every day I went
Watching its growth and wondering;
And as the day grew hot, methought I saw
A glassy vapour dancing on the pool,
And on it little quaint and filmy shapes,
With dizzy motion, wheel and rise and fall,
Like clouds of gnats with perfect lineaments.

  * * * * *

1822.

ORPHEUS.

[No trace of this poem appears in Shelley's note-books; it exists only in a transcript by Mrs. Shelley, who has written, in playful allusion to her toils as an amanuensis, "*Aspetto fin che il diluvio cala, ed allora cerco di posare argine alle sue parole;*" "I await the descent of the flood, and then I endeavour to embank his words."

From this circumstance, as well as from the internal evidence of the piece, I should conjecture that it was an attempt at *improvisation*. Shelley had several times heard Sgricci, the renowned *improvvisatore*, in the winter of 1820, and this may have inspired him with the idea of attempting a similar feat. Assuredly, this poem, though containing many felicitous passages, hardly attains his usual standard, either of thought or expression. It *may* be a translation from the Italian.]

A.

Not far from hence. From yonder pointed hills,
Crowned with a ring of oak, you may behold
A dark and barren field, through which there flows,
Sluggish and black, a deep but narrow stream,
Which the wind ripples not, and the fair moon
Gazes in vain, and finds no mirror there.
Follow the herbless banks of that strange brook

Until you pause beside a darksome pond,
The fountain of this rivulet, whose gush
Cannot be seen, hid by a rayless night
That lives beneath the overhanging rock
That shades the pool—an endless spring of gloom,
Upon whose edge hovers the tender light,
Trembling to mingle with its paramour,—
But, as Syrinx fled Pan, so night flies day.
On one side of this jagged and shapeless hill
There is a cave, from which there eddies up
A pale mist, like aërial gossamer,
Whose breath destroys all life—awhile it veils
The rock—then, scattered by the wind, it flies
Along the stream, or lingers on the clefts.
Upon the beetling edge of that dark rock
There stands a group of cypresses; not such
As, with a graceful spire and stirring life,
Pierce the pure heaven of your native vale,
Whose branches the air plays among, but not
Disturbs, fearing to spoil their solemn grace;
But blasted and all wearily these stand,
One to another clinging; their weak boughs
Sigh as the wind buffets them, and they shake
Beneath its blasts—a weather-beaten crew!

CHORUS.

What wondrous sound is that, mournful and faint,

But more melodious than the murmuring wind
That through the columns of a temple glides?

A.

It is the wandering voice of Orpheus' lyre,
Borne by the winds, who sigh that their rude king
Hurries them fast from these air-feeding notes;
But in their speed they bear along with them
The waning sound, scattering it like dew
Upon the startled sense.

CHORUS.

      Does he still sing?
Methought he rashly cast away his harp
When he had lost Eurydice.

A.

       Alas!
In times long past, when fair Eurydice
With her bright eyes sat listening by his side,
He gently sang of high and heavenly themes.
As in a brook, fretted with little waves,
By the light airs of spring—each riplet makes
A many-sided mirror for the sun,
While it flows musically through green banks,
Ceaseless and pauseless, ever clear and fresh,
So flowed his song, reflecting the deep joy

And tender love that fed those sweetest notes.
But that is past.   Returning from drear Hell,
He chose a lonely seat of unhewn stone,
Blackened with lichens, on a herbless plain.
Then from the deep and overflowing spring
Of his eternal ever-moving grief
There rose to Heaven a sound of angry song.
'Tis as a mighty cataract that parts
Two sister rocks with waters swift and strong,
And casts itself with horrid roar and din
Adown a steep; from a perennial source
It ever flows and falls, and breaks the air
With loud and fierce, but most harmonious roar,
And as it falls casts up a vaporous spray
Which the sun clothes in hues of Iris light.
Thus the tempestuous torrent of his grief
Is clothed in sweetest sounds and varying words
Of poesy.   Unlike all human works,
It never slackens, and through every change
Wisdom and beauty and the power divine
Of mighty poesy together dwell,
Mingling in sweet accord.   As I have seen
A fierce south blast tear through the darkened sky,
Driving along a rack of wingèd clouds,
Which may not pause, but ever hurry on,
As their wild shepherd wills them, whilst the stars,
Twinkling and dim, peep from between their plumes.

Anon the sky is cleared, and the high dome
Of serene Heaven, starred with its fiery flowers,
Shuts in the shaken earth ; or the still moon
Swiftly, yet gracefully, begins her walk,
Rising all bright behind the eastern hills.
I talk of moon, and wind, and stars, and not
Of song ; but would I echo his high song,
Nature must lend me words ne'er used before,
Or I must borrow from her perfect works,
To image forth his perfect attributes.
He does no longer sit upon his throne
Of rock upon a desert herbless plain,
For the evergreen and knotted ilexes,
And cypresses that seldom wave their boughs,
And sea-green olives with their grateful fruit,
And elms dragging along the twisted vines,
Which drop their berries as they follow fast,
And blackthorn bushes with their infant race
Of blushing rose blooms ; beeches, to lovers dear,
And weeping willows, too ; all swift or slow,
As their long boughs or lighter dress permit,
Have circled in his throne, and Earth herself
Has sent from her maternal breast a growth
Of starry flowers and herbs of odour sweet,
To pave the temple that his poesy
Has framed, while near his feet grim lions couch,
And kids, fearless from love, creep near his lair.

Even the blind worms seem to feel the sound.
The birds are silent, hanging down their heads,
Perched on the lowest branches of the trees;
Not even the nightingale intrudes a note
In rivalry, but all entranced she listens.

1820.

SCENE FROM TASSO.

["I have devoted," Shelley wrote from Milan, April 20, 1818, " this summer, and indeed the next year, to the composition of a tragedy on the subject of Tasso's madness ; which I find upon inspection is, if properly treated, admirably dramatic and poetical."

Brief and slight as the following fragment is, it is highly interesting, as affording some clue to the manner in which Shelley would have treated a subject which he long meditated, and never, perhaps, finally abandoned. It would appear that the envy of courtiers and Tasso's rivals would have been among the principal elements of the action ; the piece would consequently have borne little resemblance to Goethe's "Tasso," which it is doubtful whether Shelley ever read. No subject could have been more congenial to the latter. He was probably withheld from attempting it by the appearance of Byron's "Lament of Tasso," and his reluctance to enter into apparent competition with a friend, to whose genius his modesty, confirmed by the unanimous voice of his contemporaries, induced him to assign an unmerited pre-eminence over his own.]

| MADDALO | . . | *a Courtier.* | PIGNA | . . | *a Minister.* |
| MALPIGLIO | . . | *a Poet.* | ALBANO | . . | *an Usher.* |

Mad. No access to the Duke! You have not said
That the Count Maddalo would speak with him?

Pigna. Did you inform his Grace that Signor Pigna
Waits with state papers for his signature?

Mal. The Lady Leonora cannot know
That I have written a sonnet to her fame,
In which I   Venus and Adonis.
You should not take my gold and serve me not.
   Alb. In truth I told her, and she smiled and said,
" If I am Venus, thou, coy Poesy
Art the Adonis whom I love, and he
The Erymanthian boar that wounded him."
O trust to me, Signor Malpiglio,
Those nods and smiles were favours worth the zechin.
   Mal. The words are twisted in some double sense
That I reach not: the smiles fell not on me.
   Pigna. How are the Duke and Duchess occupied?
   Alb. Buried in some strange talk. The Duke was
        leaning
His finger on his brow, his lips unclosed.
The Princess sate within the window-seat,
And so her face was hid; but on her knee
Her hands were clasped, veinèd, and pale as snow,
And quivering—young Tasso, too, was there.
   Mad. Thou seest on whom from thine own worshipped heaven
Thou drawest down smiles—they did not rain on thee.
   Mal. Would they were parching lightnings for his sake
On whom they fell!

FIORDISPINA.

[SHELLEY has unconsciously afforded a key to the inmost sentiment of his writings in his "Fragment on Love," when he says:—"It is that powerful attraction towards all that we conceive, or fear, or hope beyond ourselves when we find within our own thoughts the chasm of an insufficient void, and seek to awake in all things that are a community with what we experience within ourselves . . . We are born into the world, and there is something within us which, from the instant that we live, more and more thirsts after its likeness . . . We dimly see within our intellectual nature a miniature, as it were, of our entire self, yet deprived of all that we condemn or despise, the ideal prototype of everything excellent or lovely that we are capable of conceiving as belonging to the nature of man. Not only the portrait of our external being, but an assemblage of the minutest particles of which our nature is composed; a mirror, whose surface reflects only the forms of purity and brightness; a soul within our soul, that describes a circle around its proper paradise, which pain, and sorrow, and evil dare not overleap. To this we eagerly refer all sensations, thirsting that they should resemble or correspond with it." This ideal and unearthly self—this ethereal embodiment of an unattainable perfection—this Ianthe, Laon, Laone, Lionel, Prometheus, Beatrice, or Emilia—πολλων ονοματων μορφη μια—is the presiding genius of Shelley's writings, to which almost every verse he ever penned is directly or indirectly consecrated. It is at once the cause of the transcendent beauty of these works, and of their limited acceptance; for while, on the one hand, it in a manner lifts the poet above himself, and detains him in a region of supreme purity and splendour, it, on the other hand, demands the reader's appreciation of a character by so much the more ethereal and remote from ordinary experience than even Shelley's own, as by so much the more divested of the earthly taints and clogs that beset the purest "actors in the world's great business." Shelley's poetry, in a word, is the idealised representation of Shelley himself; and hence it may be said, with strict truth, that the enjoyment of the former is an indispensable qualification for the intelligence of the latter—a Shibboleth which would have stuck in the throats of many who have taken upon themselves to judge him. This ideal tendency, gathering beauty with every successive manifestation, finally culminated in the "radiant mysticism and rapturous melody," * of "Epipsychidion," beyond which progress hardly seems possible. "Fiordispina," and the piece which I have ventured to entitle "To his Genius" (using the latter word in the sense of δαιμων), may be regarded as preliminary, though unconscious studies for this crowning work. This is indicated by the general similarity among the three, as well as by the fact that very many lines now found in "Epipsychidion" have been transferred to it from the others. Most of these have been omitted from the poems as now published; but some instances will be observed in the second, which was probably the earlier in point of date. "Fiordispina" seems to have been written during the first days of Shelley's acquaintance with Emilia Viviani, who is also the Ginevra of the poem thus entitled. Portions of both pieces have already been published, and are here inclosed within brackets.]

THE season was the childhood of sweet June,
Whose sunny hours from morning until noon
Went creeping through the day with silent feet,
Each with its load of pleasure, slow yet sweet;

* "Shelley Memorials," p. 149.

Like the long years of blest Eternity
Never to be developed. Joy to thee,
Fiordispina, and thy Cosimo,
For thou the wonders of the depth canst know
Of this unfathomable flood of hours,
Sparkling beneath the heaven which embowers—

  * * * * *

[They were two cousins, almost like two twins,
Except that from the catalogue of sins
Nature had rased their love, which could not be
But by dissevering their nativity.
And so they grew together like two flowers
Upon one stem, which the same beams and showers
Lull or awaken in their purple prime,
Which the same hand will gather—the same clime
Shake with decay. This fair day smiles to see
All those who love—and whoe'er loved like thee,
Fiordispina? Scarcely Cosimo,
Within whose bosom and whose brain now glow
The ardours of a vision which obscure
The very idol of its portraiture.
He faints, dissolved into a sea of love;
But thou art as a planet sphered above;
But thou art Love itself—ruling the motion
Of his subjected spirit: such emotion

Must end in sin or sorrow, if sweet May
Had not brought forth this morn, your wedding-day.]
* * * * *
Lie there; sleep awhile in your own dew,
Ye faint-eyed children of the   Hours,
Fiordispina said, and threw the flowers
Which she had from the breathing—

—A table near of polished porphyry.
They seemed to wear a beauty from the eye
That looked on them—a fragrance from the touch
Whose warmth   checked their life; a light such
As sleepers wear, lulled by the voice they love,
         which did reprove
The childish pity that she felt for them,
And a   remorse that from their stem
She had divided such fair shapes   made
A feeling in the   which was a shade
Of gentle beauty on the flowers: there lay
All gems that make the earth's dark bosom gay.
     rods of myrtle-buds and lemon-blooms,
And that leaf tinted lightly which assumes
The livery of unremembered snow—
Violets whose eyes have drunk—
* * * * *
Fiordispina and her nurse are now
Upon the steps of the high portico;

Under the withered arm of Media
She flings her glowing arm

  * * * * *

    step by step and stair by stair,
That withered woman, grey and white and brown—
More like a trunk by lichens overgrown
Than anything which once could have been human.
And ever as she goes the palsied woman

  * * * * *

" How slow and painfully you seem to walk,
Poor Media! you tire yourself with talk."
      " And well it may,
Fiordispina, dearest—well-a-day!
You are hastening to a marriage-bed;
I to the grave!"—"And if my love were dead,
Unless my heart deceives me, I would lie
Beside him in my shroud as willingly
As now in the gay night-dress Lilla wrought."
" Fie, child ! Let that unseasonable thought
Not be remembered till it snows in June;
Such fancies are a music out of tune
With the sweet dance your heart must keep to-night.
What! would you take all beauty and delight
Back to the Paradise from which you sprung,
And leave to grosser mortals ?———
And say, sweet lamb, would you not learn the sweet
And subtle mystery by which spirits meet?

Who knows whether the loving game is played,
When, once of mortal [vesture] disarrayed,
The naked soul goes wandering here and there
Through the wide deserts of Elysian air?
The violet dies not till it "———

   ✣   ✣   ✣   ✣   ✣

1820.

TO HIS GENIUS.

[HERE, my dear friend, is a new book for you;
I have already dedicated two
To other friends, one female and one male,*—
What you are is a thing that I must veil;
What can this be to those who praise or rail?
I never was attached to that great sect
Whose doctrine is that each one should select
Out of the world a mistress or a friend,
And all the rest, though fair and wise, commend
To cold oblivion—though 'tis in the code
Of modern morals, and the beaten road
Which those poor slaves with weary footsteps tread
Who travel to their home among the dead
By the broad highway of the world—and so
With one sad friend, and many a jealous foe,
The dreariest and the longest journey go.

Free love has this, different from gold and clay,
That to divide is not to take away.

* The " Revolt of Islam" to Mrs. Shelley, and the "Cenci" to Leigh Hunt.

Like ocean, which the general north wind breaks
Into ten thousand waves, and each one makes
A mirror of the moon—like some great glass,
Which did distort whatever form might pass,
Dashed into fragments by a playful child,
Which then reflects its eyes and forehead mild;
Giving for one, which it could ne'er express,
A thousand images of loveliness.

If I were one whom the loud world held wise,
I should disdain to quote authorities
In commendation of this kind of love :—
Why there is first the God in heaven above,
Who wrote a book called Nature, 'tis to be
Reviewed, I hear, in the next *Quarterly;*
And Socrates, the Jesus Christ of Greece;
And Jesus Christ himself did never cease
To urge all living things to love each other,
And to forgive their mutual faults, and smother
The Devil of disunion in their souls.]

  * * * * *

I love you!—Listen, O embodied Ray
Of the great Brightness; I must pass away
While you remain, and these light words must be
Tokens by which you may remember me.
Start not—the thing you are is unbetrayed,

If you are human, and if but the shade
Of some sublimer Spirit.

* * * * *

And as to friend or mistress, 'tis a form ;
Perhaps I wish you were one. Some declare
You a familiar spirit, as you are ;
Others with a   more inhuman
Hint that, though not my wife, you are a woman,
What is the colour of your eyes and hair ?
Why, if you were a lady, it were fair
The world should know—but, as I am afraid
The *Quarterly* would bait you if betrayed ;
And if, as it will be sport to see them stumble
Over all sorts of scandals, hear them mumble
Their litany of curses—some guess right,
And others swear you're a Hermaphrodite,
Like that sweet marble monster of both sexes,
With looks so sweet and gentle that it vexes
The very soul that the soul is gone
Which lifted from her limbs the veil of stone.

* * * * *

[It is a sweet thing, friendship, a dear balm,
A happy and auspicious bird of calm,
Which rides o'er life's ever tumultuous ocean,
A God that broods o'er chaos in commotion ;

TO HIS GENIUS.

A flower which fresh as Lapland roses are,
Lifts its bold head into the world's pure air,
And blooms most radiantly when others die,
Health, hope, and youth, and brief prosperity;
And with the light and odour of its bloom,
Shining within the dungeon and the tomb;
Whose coming is as light and music are
'Mid dissonance and gloom—a star
Which moves not 'mid the moving heavens alone—
A smile among dark frowns—a gentle tone
Among rude voices, a belovèd light,
A solitude, a refuge, a delight.
If I had but a friend! Why, I have three
Even by my own confession; there may be
Some more, for what I know, for 'tis my mind
To call my friends all who are wise and kind,—
And these, Heaven knows, at best are very few;
But none can ever be more dear than you.
Why should they be? My muse has lost her wings,
Or like a dying swan who soars and sings,
I should describe you in heroic style,
But as it is, are you not void of guile?
A lovely soul, formed to be blest and bless;
A well of sealed and secret happiness;
A lute which those whom Love has taught to play
Make music on to cheer the roughest day,]
And enchant sadness till it sleeps?

*   *   *   *   *

TO HIS GENIUS.

To the oblivion whither I and thou,
All loving and all lovely, hasten now
With steps, ah, too unequal! may we meet
In one Elysium or one winding-sheet!

If any should be curious to discover
Whether to you I am a friend or lover,
Let them read Shakspeare's sonnets, taking thence
A whetstone for their dull intelligence
That tears and will not cut, or let them guess
How Diotima, the wise prophetess,
Instructed the instructor, and why he
Rebuked the infant spirit of melody
On Agathon's sweet lips, which as he spoke
Was as the lovely star when morn has broke
The roof of darkness, in the golden dawn,
Half-hidden, and yet beautiful.
       I'll pawn
My hopes of Heaven—you know what they are worth—
That the presumptuous pedagogues of Earth,
If they could tell the riddle offered here
Would scorn to be, or being to appear
What now they seem and are—but let them chide,
They have few pleasures in the world beside;
Perhaps we should be dull were we not chidden,
Paradise fruits are sweetest when forbidden.
Folly can season Wisdom, Hatred Love.
  * * * * *

TO HIS GENIUS.

Farewell, if it can be to say farewell
To those who—

      *   *   *   *   *

I will not, as most dedicators do,
Assure myself and all the world and you,
That you are faultless—would to God they were
Who taunt me with your love! I then should wear
These heavy chains of life with a light spirit,
And would to God I were, or even as near it
As you, dear heart. Alas! what are we? Clouds
Driven by the wind in warring multitudes,
Which rain into the bosom of the earth,
And rise again, and in our death and birth,
And through our restless life, take as from heaven
Hues which are not our own, but which are given,
And then withdrawn, and with inconstant glance
Flash from the spirit to the countenance.
There is a Power, a Love, a Joy, a God
Which makes in mortal hearts its brief abode,
A Pythian exhalation, which inspires
Love, only love—a wind which o'er the wires
Of the soul's giant harp—
There is a mood which language faints beneath;
You feel it striding, as Almighty Death
His bloodless steed.

                                                  1820.

LOVE, HOPE, DESIRE, AND FEAR.

* * * * *

AND many there were hurt by that strong boy,
   His name, they said, was Pleasure,
And near him stood, glorious beyond measure,
Four Ladies who possess all empery.
   In earth and air and sea,
Nothing that lives from their award is free.
   Their names will I declare to thee,
   Love, Hope, Desire, and Fear,
   And they the regents are
Of the four elements that frame the heart,
And each diversely exercised her art
   By force or circumstance or sleight
     To prove her dreadful might
     Upon that poor domain.
Desire presented her [false] glass, and then
     The spirit dwelling there
Was spell-bound to embrace what seemed so fair
     Within that magic mirror,
     And dazed by that bright error,

It would have scorned the [shafts] of the avenger,
    And death, and penitence, and danger,
        Had not then silent Fear
        Touched with her palsying spear,
    So that as if a frozen torrent
    The blood was curdled in its current;
It dared not speak, even in look or motion,
But chained within itself its proud devotion.
    Between Desire and Fear thou wert
    A wretched thing, poor heart!
Sad was his life who bore thee in his breast,
    Wild bird for that weak nest.
Till Love even from fierce Desire it bought,
And from the very wound of tender thought
Drew solace, and the pity of sweet eyes
Gave strength to bear those gentle agonies,
Surmount the loss, the terror, and the sorrow.
    Then Hope approached, she who can borrow
    For poor to-day, from rich to-morrow,
    And Fear withdrew, as night when day
    Descends upon the orient ray,
    And after long and vain endurance
    The poor heart woke to her assurance.
    —At one birth these four were born
    With the world's forgotten morn,
    And from Pleasure still they hold
    All it circles, as of old.

When, as summer lures the swallow,
Pleasure lures the heart to follow—
O weak heart of little wit!
The fair hand that wounded it,
Seeking, like a panting hare,
Refuge in the lynx's lair,
Love, Desire, Hope, and Fear,
　　Ever will be near.

　　　　　　　　　　　　1821.

LINES.

We meet not as we parted,
   We feel more than all may see,
My bosom is heavy-hearted,
   And thine full of doubt for me.
   One moment has bound the free.

That moment is gone for ever,
   Like lightning that flashed and died,
Like a snowflake upon the river,
   Like a sunbeam upon the tide,
   Which the dark shadows hide.

That moment from time was singled
   As the first of a life of pain,
The cup of its joy was mingled
   —Delusion too sweet though vain!
   Too sweet to be mine again.

Sweet lips, could my heart have hidden
  That its life was crushed by you,
Ye would not have then forbidden
  The death which a heart so true
  Sought in your briny dew.

  Methinks too little cost
  For a moment so found, so lost!

1822.

LINES WRITTEN IN THE BAY OF LERICI.

She left me at the silent time
When the moon had ceased to climb
The azure path of heaven's steep,
And, like an albatross asleep,
Balanced on her wings of light,
Hovered in the purple night,
Ere she sought her ocean nest
In the chambers of the west.
She left me, and I stayed alone,
Thinking over every tone,
Which, though silent to the ear,
The enchanted heart could hear,
Like notes which die when born, but still
Haunt the echoes of the hill,
And feeling ever—O, too much!—
The soft vibration of her touch,
As if her gentle hand even now
Lightly trembled on my brow,
And thus, although she absent were,

Memory gave me all of her
That even Fancy dares to claim :—
Her presence had made weak and tame
All passions, and I lived alone
In the time which is our own ;
The past and future were forgot,
As they had been, and would be, not ;
But soon, the guardian angel gone,
The dæmon reassumed his throne
In my faint heart. I dare not speak
My thoughts ; but thus disturbed and weak
I sat, and saw the vessels glide
Over the ocean bright and wide
Like spirit-winged chariots sent
O'er some serenest element,
For ministrations strange and far,
As if to some Elysian star,
Sailed for drink to medicine
Such sweet and bitter pain as mine.
And the wind that winged their flight
From the land came fresh and light ;
And the scent of wingèd flowers,
And the coolness of the hours
Of dew, and sweet warmth left by day,
Were scattered o'er the twinkling bay,
And the fisher, with his lamp
And spear, about the low rocks damp

Crept, and struck the fish which came
To worship the delusive flame.
Too happy they, whose pleasure sought,
Extinguishes all sense and thought
Of the regret that pleasure leaves,
Destroying life alone, not peace!

                      1822.

FRAGMENTS OF THE ADONAIS.

[AMONG Shelley's MSS. is a fair copy of the "Defence of Poetry," apparently damaged by sea-water, and illegible in many places. Being prepared for the printer, it is written on one side of the paper only; on the blank pages, but frequently undecipherable for the reason just indicated, are many passages intended for, but eventually omitted from, the preface to "Adonais." Their autobiographical value requires no comment.]

. . . The expression of my indignation and sympathy. I will allow myself a first and last word on the subject of calumny as it relates to me. As an author I have dared and invited censure. If I understand myself, I have written neither for profit nor for fame. I have employed my poetical compositions and publications simply as the instruments of that sympathy between myself and others which the ardent and unbounded love I cherished for my kind incited me to acquire. I expected all sorts of stupidity and insolent contempt from those . . .

. . . These compositions (excepting the tragedy

of the " Cenci," which was written rather to try my powers, than to unburthen my full heart) are insufficiently . . . commendation than perhaps they deserve, even from their bitterest enemies; but they have not attained any corresponding popularity. As a man, I shrink from notice and regard; the ebb and flow of the world vexes me; I desire to be left in peace. Persecution, contumely, and calumny, have been heaped upon me in profuse measure; and domestic conspiracy and legal oppression have violated in my person the most sacred rights of nature and humanity. The bigot will say it was the recompence of my errors; the man of the world will call it the result of my imprudence; but never upon one head . . .

. . . Reviewers, with some rare exceptions, are a most stupid and malignant race. As a bankrupt thief turns thieftaker in despair, so an unsuccessful author turns critic. But a young spirit panting for fame, doubtful of its powers, and certain only of its aspirations, is ill-qualified to assign its true value to the sneer of this world. He knows not that such stuff as this is of the abortive and monstrous births which time consumes as fast as it produces. He sees the truth and falsehood, the merits and demerits, of his case inextricably entangled . . . No personal offence should have drawn from me this public comment upon such stuff . . .

. . . The offence of this poor victim * seems to have consisted solely in his intimacy with Leigh Hunt, Mr. Hazlitt, and some other enemies of despotism and superstition. My friend Hunt has a very hard skull to crack, and will take a deal of killing. I do not know much of Mr. Hazlitt, but . . .

. . . I knew personally but little of Keats; but on the news of his situation I wrote to him, suggesting the propriety of trying the Italian climate, and inviting him to join me. Unfortunately he did not allow me . . .

[Several cancelled passages of the "Adonais" have been met with in Shelley's note-books. He appears to have originally framed his conception on a larger scale than he eventually found practicable. The passage in which the contemporary minstrels are introduced as mourning for Adonais, would have been considerably extended, and the characteristics of each delineated at some length. It must, however, have occurred to him that the parenthesis would be too long, and would tend to distract the reader's attention from the main subject. Nothing, therefore, of the original draft was allowed to subsist, but the four incomparable stanzas descriptive of himself ("Mid others of less note," &c.). A fifth was cancelled, which ran as follows :—]

> And ever as he went he swept a lyre
> Of unaccustomed shape, and   strings

---

* It is hardly necessary to repeat what Mr. Milnes has so clearly established, that Shelley very greatly overrated the effect which the Quarterly's attack produced upon Keats. The error, however, was almost universal at the time.

Now like the   of impetuous fire,
Which shakes the forest with its murmurings,
Now like the rush of the aerial wings
Of the enamoured wind among the treen,
Whispering unimaginable things,
And dying on the streams of dew serene,
Which feed the unmown meads with ever-during
green.

[Several stanzas relating to Byron and Moore are too imperfect for publication. The following refers to the latter:—]

And the green Paradise which western waves
Embosom in their ever-wailing sweep,
Talking of freedom to their tongueless caves,
Or to the spirits which within them keep
A record of the wrongs which, though they sleep,
Die not, but dream of retribution, heard
His hymns, and echoing them from steep to steep,
Kept—

[Leigh Hunt was thus described:—]

And then came one of sweet and earnest looks,
Whose soft smiles to his dark and night-like eyes
Were as the clear and ever-living brooks
Are to the obscure fountains whence they rise,
Showing how pure they are: a Paradise

Of happy truth upon his forehead low
Lay, making wisdom lovely, in the guise
Of earth-awakening morn upon the brow
Of star-deserted heaven, while ocean gleams below.

His song, though very sweet, was low and faint,
A simple strain———

———

[The following lines were also written for the "Adonais":—]

      A mighty Phantasm, half concealed
In darkness of his own exceeding light,
Which clothed his awful presence unrevealed,
Charioted on the   night
Of thunder-smoke, whose skirts were chrysolite.

And like a sudden meteor, which outstrips
The splendour-winged chariot of the sun,
           eclipse
The armies of the golden stars, each one
Pavilioned in its tent of light—all strewn
Over the chasms of blue night ———

TRANSLATION OF THE FIRST CANZONE OF DANTE'S CONVITO.*

Ye who intelligent the third heaven move,
Hear the discourse which is within my heart,
Which cannot be declared, it seems so new;
The Heaven whose course follows your power and art,
O gentle creatures that ye are! me drew,
And therefore may I dare to speak to you,
Even of the life which now I live—and yet
I pray that ye will hear me when I cry,
And tell of mine own heart this novelty;
How the lamenting spirit moans in it,
And how a voice there murmurs against her
Who came on the refulgence of your sphere.

A sweet thought, which was once the life within
This heavy heart, many a time and oft
Went up before our Father's feet, and there
It saw a glorious Lady † throned aloft;

---

* Voi che intendendo il terzo ciel movete, &c.
† Beatrice.

And its sweet talk of her my soul did win,
So that I said, Thither I too will fare.
That thought is fled, and one doth now appear
Which tyrannises me with such fierce stress,
That my heart trembles—ye may see it leap—
And on another Lady* bids me keep
Mine eyes, and says—who would have blessedness
Let him but look upon that lady's eyes,
Let him not fear the agony of sighs.

This lowly thought, which once would talk with me
Of a bright seraph sitting crowned on high,
Found such a cruel foe it died, and so
My spirit wept, the grief is hot even now—
And said, Alas for me! how swift could flee
That piteous thought which did my life console!
And the afflicted one   questioning
Mine eyes, if such a lady saw they never,
And why they would
I said, beneath those eyes might stand for ever
He whom   regards must kill with
To have known their power stood me in little stead,
Those eyes have looked on me, and I am dead.

Thou art not dead, but thou hast wanderèd,
Thou soul of ours, who thyself dost fret,

         * Philosophy.

A spirit of gentle love beside me said;
For that fair lady, whom thou dost regret,
Hath so transformed the life which thou hast led,
Thou scornest it, so worthless art thou made.
And see how meek, how pitiful, how staid,
Yet courteous, in her majesty she is.
And still call thou her woman in thy thought;
Her whom, if thou thyself deceivest not,
Thou wilt behold decked with such loveliness,
That thou wilt cry [Love] only Lord, lo here
Thy handmaiden,* do what thou wilt with her.

My song, I fear that thou wilt find but few
Who fitly shall conceive thy reasoning
Of such hard matter dost thou entertain.
Whence, if by misadventure chance should bring
Thee to base company, as chance may do,
Quite unaware of what thou dost contain,
I prithee comfort thy sweet self again,
My last delight; tell them that they are dull,
And bid them own that thou art beautiful.†

1820.

* Soul being feminine in Italian.
† This last stanza was subsequently published as an introduction to "Epipsychidion."

MATILDA GATHERING FLOWERS.

[From the "Purgatorio" of Dante, cant. 28, l. 1-51. Part of it has already been published in Medwin's "Life of Shelley," vol. ii., pp. 16, 18.]

AND earnest to explore within—around
The divine wood, whose thick green living woof
Tempered the young day to the sight—I wound

Up the green slope, beneath the forest's roof,
With slow soft steps leaving the mountain's steep,
And sought those inmost labyrinths, motion-proof

Against the air, that in that stillness deep
And solemn, struck upon my forehead bare,
The slow soft stroke of a continuous

In which the   leaves tremblingly were
All bent towards that part where earliest
The sacred hill obscures the morning air.

Yet were they not so shaken from the rest,
But that the birds, perched on the utmost spray,
Incessantly renewing their blithe quest,

With perfect joy received the early day,
Singing within the glancing leaves, whose sound
Kept a low burden to their roundelay,

Such as from bough to bough gathers around
The pine forest on bleak Chiassi's shore,
When Æolus Sirocco has unbound.

My slow steps had already borne me o'er
Such space within the antique wood, that I
Perceived not where I entered any more,

When, lo! a stream whose little waves went by,
Bending towards the left through grass that grew
Upon its bank, impeded suddenly

My going on. Water of purest hue
On earth, would appear turbid and impure
Compared with this, whose unconcealing dew,

Dark, dark, yet clear, moved under the obscure
Eternal shades, whose interwoven looms
The rays of moon or sunlight ne'er endure.

I moved not with my feet, but 'mid the glooms
Pierced with my charmed eye contemplating
The mighty multitude of fresh May blooms

That starred that night, when, even as a thing
That suddenly for blank astonishment
Dissolves all other thought,

A solitary woman! and she went
Singing and gathering flower after flower,
With which her way was painted and besprent.

Bright lady, who, if looks had ever power
To bear true witness of the heart within,
Dost bask under the beams of love, come lower

Towards this bank. I prithee let me win
This much of thee, to come, that I may hear
Thy song—like Proserpine in Enna's glen.

Thou seemest to my fancy, singing here
And gathering flowers, as that fair maiden when
She lost the spring, and Ceres her more dear.

1820.

TRANSLATION OF
HOMER'S HYMN TO VENUS.

[V. 1-55, with some omissions.]

MUSE, sing the deeds of golden Aphrodite,
Who wakens with her smile the lulled delight
Of sweet desire, taming the eternal kings
Of Heaven, and men, and all the living things
That fleet along the air, or whom the sea,
Or earth with her maternal ministry
Nourish innumerable, thy delight
All seek   O crowned Aphrodite.
Three spirits canst thou not deceive or quell,
Minerva, child of Jove, who loves too well
Fierce war and mingling combat, and the fame
Of glorious deeds, to heed thy gentle flame.
Diana,   golden-shafted queen,
Is tamed not by thy smiles; the shadows green
Of the wild woods, the bow, the
And piercing cries amid the swift pursuit
Of beasts among waste mountains, such delight
Is hers, and men who know and do the right.

Nor Saturn's first-born daughter, Vesta chaste,
Whom Neptune and Apollo wooed the last,
Such was the will of ægis-bearing Jove,
But sternly she refused the ills of Love,
And by her mighty father's head she swore
An oath not unperformed, that evermore
A virgin she would live 'mid deities
Divine : her father, for such gentle ties
Renounced, gave glorious gifts, thus in his hall
She sits and feeds luxuriously, o'er all
In every fane, her honours first arise
From men—the eldest of Divinities.

These spirits she persuades not, nor deceives,
But none beside escape, so well she weaves
Her unseen toils; nor mortal men, nor gods
Who live secure in their unseen abodes.
She won the soul of him whose fierce delight
Is thunder—first in glory and in might.
And, as she willed, his mighty mind deceiving,
With mortal limbs his deathless limbs inweaving,
Concealed him from his spouse and sister fair,
Whom to wise Saturn ancient Rhea bare.

        but in return,
In Venus Jove did soft desire awaken,
That by her own enchantments overtaken,

She might, no more from human union free,
Burn for a nursling of mortality.
For once, amid the assembled Deities,
The laughter-loving Venus from her eyes
Shot forth the light of a soft starlight smile,
And boasting said, that she, secure the while,
Could bring at will to the assembled gods
The mortal tenants of earth's dark abodes,
And mortal offspring from a deathless stem
She could produce in scorn and spite of them.
Therefore he poured desire into her breast
Of young Anchises,
Feeding his herds among the mossy fountains
Of the wide Ida's many-folded mountains,
Whom Venus saw, and loved, and the love clung
Like wasting fire her senses wild among.

1818.

UNA FAVOLA.

C'era un giovane il quale viaggiava per paesi lontani, cercando per il mondo una donna, della quale esso fu innamorato. E chi fu quella donna, e come questo giovane s'innamorò di lei, e come e perchè gli cessò l'amore tanto forte che aveva, sono cose degne d'essere conosciute da ogni gentil cuore.

Al spuntare della decima quinta primavera della sua vita, uno chiamandosi Amore gli destava, dicendo che una chi egli aveva molte volte veduto nei sogni gli stava aspettando. Quello fu accompagnato d'una schiera immensa di persone, tutte velate in bianchi veli, e coronate di lauro, ellera e mirto inghirlandite ed intrecciate di viole, rose, e fiordilisi. Cantavano si dolcemente che forse l'armonia delle sfere alla quale le stelle ballano, e meno soave. E le maniere e le parole loro erano cosi lusinghevoli, che il giovane fu allettato, e levandosi del letto, si fece pronto di fare tutto il volere di quello che si chiamava Amore, al di cui cenno lo seguitava per solinghe vie ed eremi e caverne, fino che tutta la schiera arrivò ad un bosco solitario in una cupa valle per due altissime montagne, il quale fu piantato a guisa di laberinto di pini, cipressi, cedari e tassi, le ombre dei quali destavano un misto di diletto e malinconia. Ed in questo bosco il giovane seguitava per un anno intero i passi incerti di questo compagno e duce suo, come la luna segue la terra; non però tramutandosi come essa. E fu egli nutrito delle fruttà d'un certo albero che crebbe nel mezzo del laberinto, un cibo insieme dolce ed amaro, il quale essendo freddo come ghiaccio sulle labbre, pareva fuoco nelle vene. Le forme velate sempre gli furoro intorno, erano servi e ministri ubbedienti al menomo cenno, e corrieri per lui ed Amore quando per affari suoi l'Amore un poco lo lascierebbe. Ma queste forme, eseguendo ogni altra ordine sua prestamente, mai non vollero svelarsi a lui quantunque le pregasse sollecitamente; eccettuato una, che aveva nome la Vita, ed aveva riputazione di incantatrice gagliarda. Era essa grande di persona e bella, allegra e sciolta, ed ornata riccamente, e, siccome pareva dal suo pronto svelarsi, voleva bene a questo giovane. Ma ben presto la riconobbe d'essere piu finta che alcuna Sirena, poichè per consiglio suo, Amore gli lasciò in questo selvaggio luogo, colla sola compagnia di queste velate, le quali per il loro ostinato celarsi sempre gli avevano fatto qualche paura. E, sé quelle forme erano i spettri dei suoi proprii morti pensieri, ovvero le ombre dei vivi pensieri dell'Amore, nessuno può schiarire. La

Vita, vergognandosi forse della sua fraude, si celò allora dentro alla spelonca d'una sua sorella abitando colá; ed Amore se ne tornò, sospirando, alla sua terza sfera.

Appena fu partito Amore, quando le mascherate forme, solute della sua legge, si svelarono davanti all' attonito giovane. E per molti giorni le sopradette figure ballavano intorno di lui dovunque andasse—ora motteggiando ed ora minacciandolo, e la notte quando riposava sfilavano in lunga e lenta processione davanti al suo letto, ognuna più schifosa e terribile che l'altra. Il loro orribile aspetto e ria figura gli ingombrava tanto il cuore di tristezza, che il bel cielo, coperto di quella ombra, si vestì di nuvoloso tutto agli occhi suoi; e tanto pianse, che le erbe del suo cammino pasciate di lagrime in vece di rugiada, diventarono come lui, pallide e chinate. Stanco alfine di questo soffrire, veniva alla grotta della Sorella della Vita, incantatrice anch'ella, e la trovò seduta davanti un pallido fuoco di odorose legna, cantando lai soavemente dolorosi, e tessendo una bianca mortaia, sopra la quale suo nome era a mezzo intessato, con qualche altro nome oscuro ed imperfetto; ed egli la pregò di dirlo suo nome, ed ella disse con voce fiocca ma dolce—" La Morte;" ed il giovane disse—" O bella Morte, ti prego di aiutarmi contro di queste noiose immagini, compagni della tua sorella, le quali mi tormentano tutta-via." E la Morte lo rassicurò, gli prese la mano, ridendo, e gli baciò la fronte e le guancie, sicchè tremava ogni vena di gioia e di paura; e gli fece stare presso di sè, in una camera della sua grotta, dove, disse, fu contro al destino che le rie forme, compagne della Vita, venissero. Il giovane continuamente praticandosi colla Morte, ed ella, coll' animo di sorella, carezzandolo e facendo ogni cortesia di atto e di parola, ben presto s' innamorò di lei; e la Vita stessa, non che alcuna della sua schiera, non gli pareva bella. E tanto lo vinse la passione, che sul ginocchio pregò la Morte di amarlo come egli amava lei, e di voler fare il suo piacere. Ma la Morte disse, "Ardito che tu siei, al desir del quale mai ha la Morte corrisposta? Si tu non mi amasti, io forse ti amerei, amandomi io ti odio, e fuggo." Così dicendo, uscì della spelonca, e la sua oscura ed eterea figura fu presto persa fra gli intrecciati rami della selva.

Da quel punto il giovane seguiva le orme della Morte, e sì forte fu l' amore chi lo menava, che aveva circuito l' orbe, ed indagato ogni sua regione; e molti anni erano già spenti, ma le soffranze più che gli anni avevano imbiancita la chioma ed appassito il fiore della forma, quando si trovò sui confini della stessa selva della quale aveva cominciato il suo misero errare. E si gittò sull'erba, e per molte ore pianse; e le lagrime l' accecavano tanto, che per molto tempo non se n' avvidde, che tutte quelle che bagnavano il viso e il petto, non furono sue proprie; ma che una donna chinata dietro di lui pianse per pietà del suo pianto. E levando gli occhi la vidde; e mai

F

gli pareva d'aver veduto una visione si gloriosa: e dubitava forte si fosse cosa umana. Suo amore per la Morte fu improvvisamente cangiato in odio e sospetto, perche questo nuovo amore fu si forte che vinse ogni altro pensiero. E quella pietosa donna primo gli amava per pietà sola, ma tosto colla compassione crebbe l'amore; e gl'amava schiettamente, non avendo più uopo d'essere compatito alcuno amato da quella. Fu questa la donna, in traccia della quale Amore aveva menato il giovane per quel oscuro laberinto, e fatto tanto errare e soffrire; forse che lo giudicava indegno ancora di tanta gloria, e che lo vedeva debole per tolerare si immensa gioia. Dopo avere un poco asciugato il pianto, quei due passeggiavano insieme in questa stessa selva, fin chè la Morte si mise avanti e disse, "Mentre che, o giovane, mi amasti, io ti odiava, ed ora che tu mi odiasti, ti amo, e voglio tanto bene a te ed alla tua sposa che nel mio regno, che tu puoi chiamare Paradiso, ho serbato un eletto luogo, dove voi potete securamente compire i vostri felici amori." E la donna sdegnata, o forse un poco ingelosita per cagione dell' amore passato dello suo sposo, tornò il dosso sopra la Morte, dicendo fra se stesso, "Che vuol questa amante del mio sposo che viene qui turbarci?" e chiamò "Vita, Vita!" e la Vita venne col viso allegro, coronata d'una iride, e vestita in versicolore manto di pelle di cameleone, e la Morte se ni andò piangendo, e partendo disse dolcemente, "Voi mi sospettate, ma io vi lo perdono, e vi aspetto dove bisogna che passiate, perchè io abito coll' Amore e coll' Eternità, con quelle e forza che praticassero quelle anime che eternamente amano. Voi vedrete allora se io ho meritata i vostri dubbj. Intanto vi raccomando alla Vita, e, sorella mia, ti prego per amore di quella Morte della quella tu sei la gemella, di non adoperare contra di questi amanti le tue solite arti, che ti basti il tributo già pagato di sospiri e di lagrime, che sono le ricchezze tue." Il giovane, rammentandosi di quanti mali gli aveva recati in quel bosco, se disfidava della Vita ; ma la donna, quantunque in sospetto, essendo pure gelosa della Morte, . . .

[TRANSLATION.]

A FABLE.

THERE was a youth who travelled through distant lands, seeking throughout the world a lady of whom he was enamoured. And who this lady was, and how this youth became enamoured of her, and how and why the great love he bore her forsook him, are things worthy to be known by every gentle heart.

At the dawn of the fifteenth spring of his life, a certain one calling himself Love awoke him, saying that one whom he had ofttimes beheld in his dreams abode awaiting him. This Love was accompanied by a great troop of female forms, all veiled in white, and crowned with laurel, ivy, and myrtle, garlanded and interwreathed with violets, roses, and lilies. They sang with such sweetness that perhaps the harmony of the spheres, to which the stars dance, is not so sweet. And their manners and words were so alluring, that the youth was enticed, and, arising from his couch, made himself ready to do all the pleasure of him who called himself Love; at whose behest he followed him by lonely ways and deserts and caverns, until the whole troop arrived at a solitary wood, in a gloomy valley between two most lofty mountains, which valley was planted in the manner of a labyrinth, with pines, cypresses, cedars, and yews, whose shadows begot a mixture of delight and sadness. And in this wood the youth for a whole year followed the uncertain footsteps of this his companion and guide, as the moon follows the earth, save that there was no change in him, and nourished by the fruit of a certain tree which grew in the midst of the labyrinth—a food sweet and bitter at once, which being cold as ice to the lips, appeared fire in the veins. The veiled figures were continually around him, ministers and attendants obedient to his least gesture, and messengers between him and Love, when Love might leave him for a little on his other errands. But these figures, albeit executing his every other command with swiftness, never would unveil themselves to him, although he anxiously besought them; one only excepted, whose name was Life, and who had the fame of a potent enchantress. She was tall of person and beautiful, cheerful and easy in her manners, and richly adorned, and, as it seemed from her ready unveiling of herself, she wished well to this youth. But he soon perceived that she was more false than any Siren, for by her counsel Love abandoned him in this savage place, with only the company of these shrouded figures, who, by their obstinately remaining veiled, had always wrought him dread. And none can expound whether these figures were the spectres of his own dead thoughts, or the shadows of the living thoughts of Love. Then Life, haply ashamed of her deceit, concealed herself within the cavern of a certain sister of hers dwelling there; and Love, sighing, returned to his third heaven.

Scarcely had Love departed, when the masked forms, released from his government, unveiled themselves before the astonished youth. And for many days these figures danced around him whithersoever he went, alternately mocking and threatening him; and in the night while he reposed they defiled in long and slow procession before his couch, each more hideous and terrible than the other. Their horrible aspect and loathsome figure so overcame his heart with sadness that the fair heaven, covered with that shadow, clothed itself in clouds before his eyes; and he wept so much that the herbs upon his path, fed with tears instead of dew, became pale and bowed like himself. Weary at length of this suffering, he came to the grot of the Sister of Life, herself also an enchantress, and found her sitting before a pale fire of perfumed wood, singing laments sweet in their melancholy, and weaving a white shroud, upon which his name was half wrought, with the obscure and imperfect beginning of a certain other name; and he besought her to tell him her own, and she said, with a faint but sweet voice, "Death." And the youth said, "O lovely Death, I pray thee to aid me against these hateful phantoms, companions of thy sister, which cease not to torment me." And Death comforted him, and took his hand with a smile, and kissed his brow and cheek, so that every vein thrilled with joy and fear, and made him abide with her in a chamber of her cavern, whither, she said, it was against Destiny that the wicked companions of Life should ever come. The youth continually conversing with Death, and she, like-minded to a sister, caressing him and showing him every courtesy both in deed and word, he quickly became enamoured of her, and Life herself, far less any of her troop, seemed fair to him no longer: and his passion so overcame him, that upon his knees he prayed Death to love him as he loved her, and consent to do his pleasure. But Death said, "Audacious that thou art, with whose desire has Death ever complied? If thou lovedst me not, perchance I might love thee—beloved by thee, I hate thee and I fly thee." Thus saying, she went forth from the cavern, and her dusky and ethereal form was soon lost amid the interwoven boughs of the forest.

From that moment the youth pursued the track of Death; and so mighty was the love that led him, that he had encircled the world and searched through all its regions, and many years were already spent, but sorrows rather than years had blanched his locks and withered the flower of his beauty, when he found himself upon the confines of the very forest from which his wretched wanderings had begun. He cast himself upon the grass and wept for many hours, so blinded by his tears that for much time he did not perceive that not all that bathed his face and his bosom were his own, but that a lady bowed behind him wept for pity of his weeping. And lifting up his eyes he saw her, and it seemed to him never to have beheld so glorious a vision, and he doubted much whether she were a human creature. And his love of Death was suddenly changed into hate and suspicion, for this new love was so potent that it overcame every other thought. This compassionate lady at first loved him for mere pity; but love grew up swiftly with compassion, and she loved for Love's own sake, no one beloved by her having need of pity any more. This was the lady in whose quest Love had led the youth through that gloomy labyrinth of error and suffering, haply for that he esteemed him unworthy of so much glory, and perceived him too weak to support such exceeding joy. After having somewhat dried their tears, the twain walked together in that same forest, until Death stood before them, and said, "Whilst, O youth, thou didst love me, I hated thee, and now that thou hatest me, I love thee, and wish so well to thee and thy bride that in my kingdom, which thou mayest call Paradise, I have set apart a chosen spot, where ye may securely fulfil your happy loves." And the lady, offended, and perchance somewhat jealous by reason of the past love of her spouse, turned her back upon Death, saying within herself, "What would this lover of my husband who comes here to trouble us?" and cried, "Life! Life!" and Life came, with a gay visage, crowned with a rainbow, and clad in a various mantle of chameleon skin; and Death went away weeping, and departing said with a sweet voice, "Ye mistrust me, but I forgive ye, and await ye where ye needs must come, for I dwell with Love and Eternity, with whom the souls whose love is everlasting must hold communion; then will ye perceive whether I have deserved your distrust. Meanwhile I commend ye to Life; and, sister mine, I beseech thee, by the love of that Death with whom thou wert twin born, not to employ thy customary arts against these lovers, but content thee with the tribute thou hast already received of sighs and tears, which are thy wealth." The youth, mindful of how great evil she had wrought him in that wood, mistrusted Life; but the lady, although she doubted, yet being jealous of Death, . . .

1820.

MISCELLANEOUS FRAGMENTS.

I.

Dear home, thou scene of earliest hopes and joys,
The least of which wronged Memory ever makes
Bitterer than all thine unremembered tears.

1816.*

[Remarkable as the only passage in which Shelley alludes to his home.]

II.

*   *   *   *   *

A shovel of his ashes took
From the hearth's obscurest nook,
Muttering mysteries as she went.
Helen and Henry knew that granny
Was as much afraid of ghosts as any,
   And so they followed hard—
But Helen clung to her brother's arm,
And her own spasm made her shake.

1816.

[Apparently a fragment of a ghost-story. Shelley was partial to the name "Helen," as that of his favourite sister. "Henry" is the name of Ianthe's lover, in "Queen Mab."]

* The dates appended to these fragments are usually conjectural, but no important error will have been committed.

III.

There is a voice, not understood by all,
Sent from these desert-caves. It is the roar
Of the rent ice-cliff which the sunbeams call,
Plunging into the vale—it is the blast
Descending on the pines—the torrents pour . . . .

1816.

[A cancelled passage of "Mont Blanc."]

IV.

Those whom nor power, nor lying faith, nor toil,
   Nor custom, queen of many slaves, makes blind,
Have ever grieved that man should be the spoil
   Of his own weakness, and with earnest mind
Fed hopes of its redemption, these recur
   Chastened by deathful victory now, and find
Foundations in this foulest age, and stir
   Me whom they cheer to be their minister.

1817.

V.

*   *   *   *   *

For me, my friend, if not that tears did tremble
   In my faint eyes, and that my heart beat fast
With feelings which make rapture pain resemble,
   Yet, from thy voice that falsehood starts aghast,

I thank thee—let the tyrant keep
His chains and tears, yea let him weep
With rage to see thee freshly risen,
Like strength from slumber, from the prison
In which he vainly hoped the soul to bind
Which on the chains must prey that fetter humankind.

1817.

VI.

Once more descend
The shadows of my soul upon mankind,
  For to those hearts with which they never blend,
Thoughts are but shadows which the flashing mind
  From the swift clouds which track its flight of fire,
Casts on the gloomy world it leaves behind.

1817.

VII.

Dark is the realm of grief, but human things
Those may not know who cannot weep for them.

1817.

[From "Otho."]

VIII.

O that a chariot of cloud were mine!
  Of cloud which the wild tempest weaves in air,
When the moon over the ocean's line
  Is spreading the locks of her bright grey hair.

O that a chariot of cloud were mine!
I would sail on the waves of the billowy wind
To the mountain peak and the rocky lake,
And the . . . .

1817.

IX.

The wonderful description of Love in Plato, Sympos. p. 214—particularly 214, l. 8—*l. ultima, et passim* 218.

I should say in answer, that Ἔρως neither loved nor was loved, but is the cause of Love in others—a subtlety to beat Plato. *Agathon*, a poem.

1817.

X.

The world is now our dwelling-place;
Where'er the earth one fading trace
Of what was great and free does keep,
That is our home! . . . .
Mild thoughts of man's ungentle race
Shall our contented exile reap
For who that in some happy place
His own free thoughts can freely chase
By woods and waves, can clothe his face
In cynic smiles? Child! we shall weep.

1818.

[From the original draft of the verses to William Shelley, as are also the following:—]

XI.

     This lament,
  The memory of thy grievous wrong
  Will fade . . . .
   But Genius is omnipotent
  To hallow . . . .

           1818.

XII.

O mighty mind, in whose deep stream this age
Shakes like a reed in the unheeding storm,
Why dost thou curb not thine own sacred rage?

           1818.

XIII.

Silence! O well are Death and Sleep and Thou
Three brethren named, the guardians gloomy-wing'd
Of one abyss, where life, and truth, and joy
Are swallowed up—yet spare me, Spirit, pity me,
Until the sounds I hear become my soul,
And it has left these faint and weary limbs
To track along the lapses of the air
This wandering melody until it rests
Among lone mountains in some . . . . .

           1818.

XIV.

  What think you the dead are?
      Why, dust and clay,

What should they be?
                'Tis the last hour of day.
Look on the west, how beautiful it is
Vaulted with radiant vapours! The deep bliss
Of that unutterable light has made
The edges of that cloud   fade
Into a hue, like some harmonious thought,
Wasting itself on that which it had wrought,
Till it dies   and between
The light hues of the tender, pure, serene,
And infinite tranquillity of heaven.

Aye, beautiful! but when our . . . .
1818.

[This would seem to have originally formed a portion of "Julian and Maddalo," to which the next fragment may also have belonged.]

XV.

Perhaps the only comfort which remains
Is the unheeded clanking of my chains,
The which I make, and call it melody.
1818.

XVI.

The world is full of woodmen who expel
Love's gentle dryads from the haunts of life,
And vex the nightingales in every dell.
1818.

[From "The Woodman and the Nightingale."]

XVII.

Follow to the deep wood's weeds,
Follow to the wild briar dingle,
Where we sink to intermingle,
And the violet tells her tale
To the odour-scented gale,
For they two have enough to do
Of such work as I and you.

1819.

XVIII.

At the creation of the Earth
Pleasure, that divinest birth,
From the soil of Heaven did rise,
Wrapt in sweet wild melodies—
Like an exhalation wreathing
To the sound of air low-breathing
Through Æolian pines, which make
A shade and shelter to the lake
Whence it rises soft and slow;
Her life breathing [limbs] did flow
In the harmony divine
Of an ever-lengthening line
Which enwrapt her perfect form
With a beauty clear and warm.

1819.

XIX.

That famous passage in that pathetic sonnet in which, addressing a dear friend, he [Shakspeare] complains of his own situation as an actor, and says that his nature is (I quote from memory)

" Subdued
To what it works in, like the dyer's hand."

Observe these images, how simple they are, and yet animated with what intense poetry and passion.

[A note on the original MS. of the preface to "The Cenci."]

XX.

People of England, ye who toil and groan,
Who reap the harvests which are not your own,
Who weave the clothes which your oppressors wear
And for your own take the inclement air;
Who build warm houses .   .   .   .
And are like gods who give them all they have,
And nurse them from the cradle to the grave.

1819.

XXI.

I am as a spirit who has dwelt
Within his heart of hearts, and I have felt
His feelings, and have thought his thoughts, and known
The inmost converse of his soul, the tone

Unheard but in the silence of his blood,
When all the pulses in their multitude
Image the trembling calm of summer seas.
I have unlocked the golden melodies
Of his deep soul, as with a master-key,
And loosened them and bathed myself therein—
Even as an eagle in a thunder-mist
Clothing his wings with lightning.

1819.

XXII.

Is not to-day enough? Why do I peer
Into the darkness of the day to come?
Is not to-morrow even as yesterday?
And will the day that follows change thy doom?
Few flowers grow upon thy wintry way;
And who waits for thee in that cheerless home
Whence thou hast fled, whither thou must return
Charged with the load that makes thee faint and mourn?

1819.

XXIII.

Is it that in some brighter sphere
We part from friends we meet with here?
Or do we see the Future pass
Over the Present's dusky glass?

Or what is that that makes us seem
To patch up fragments of a dream,
Part of which comes true, and part
Beats and trembles in the heart?

1819.

XXIV.

[*To the Editor of the " Quarterly Review."*]

Sir,—I observe in the Sept. No. of the *Review*, which . . . . . the author of that article, after depreciating the merits of a poem written by me, asserts that what " he now knows to the disadvantage of my personal character affords an unanswerable comment on the text either of his review or my poem." I hereby call upon the author of that article, or you as the responsible agent, publicly to produce your proofs, or, as you have thrust yourself forward to deserve the character of a slanderer, to acquiesce also in . . . .

1819.

XXV.

As the sunrise to the night,
   As the north wind to the clouds,
As the earthquake's fiery flight,
   Ruining mountain solitudes,
Everlasting Italy,
Be those hopes and fears on thee.

1819.

XXVI.

Within a cavern of man's trackless spirit
Is throned an Image, so intensely fair
That the adventurous thoughts that wander near it
Worship, and as they kneel tremble and wear
The splendour of its presence, and the light
   Penetrates their dreamlike frame
Till they become charged with the strength of flame.
1820.

[A cancelled passage of the "Ode to Liberty."]

XXVII.

Such hope, as is the sick despair of good,
Such fear, as is the certainty of ill,
Such doubt, as is pale Expectation's food
Turned while she tastes to poison, when the will
Is powerless, and the spirit . . . .
1820.

XXVIII.

My head is heavy, my limbs are weary,
And it is not life that makes me move.
1820.

XXIX.

That our country is on the point of submitting to some momentous change in its internal government, is

a fact which few who observe and compare the
of human society will dispute. The distribution of
wealth, no less than the spirit by which it is upheld
and that by which it is assailed, render the event
inevitable. Call it reform or revolution, as you will, a
change must take place; one of the consequences of
which will be, the wresting of political power from
those who are at present the depositaries of it. A
strong sentiment [prevails] in the nation at large, that
they have been guilty of enormous malversations of
their trust. It is a commonplace of political reformers
to say, that it is the measures, not the men, they
abhor; and it is a general practice, so soon as the
party shall have gained the victory, to inflict the
severest punishments upon their predecessors, and to
pursue measures not less selfish and pernicious than
those, a protest against which was the ladder that
conducted them to power. The people sympathise
with the passions of their liberators, without reflecting
that these in turn may become their tyrants, and without perceiving that the same motives and excitements
to act or to feel can never, except by a perverse imitation,
belong to both.

xxx.

Unrisen splendour of the brightest sun,
To rise upon our darkness, if the star

Now beckoning thee out of thy misty throne
Could thaw the clouds which wage an obscure war
With thy young brightness!

1820.

XXXI.

Send the stars light, but send not love to me.

[The first line of an unfinished second stanza of the Madrigal to Emilia Viviani.]

XXXII.

And what is that most brief and bright delight
Which rushes through the touch and through the sight,
And stands before the spirit's inmost throne,
A naked seraph? None hath ever known.
Its birth is darkness, and its growth desire;
Untameable and fleet and fierce as fire,
Not to be touched but to be felt alone,
It fills the world with glory—and is gone.

1821.

[A cancelled passage of "Epipsychidion," as are also the three following :—]

XXXIII.

  It floats with rainbow pinions o'er the stream
    Of life, which flows, like a   dream
  Into the light of morning, to the grave
    As to an ocean.

1821.

XXXIV.

What is that joy which serene infancy
Perceives not, as the hours content them by [sic],
Each in a chain of blossoms, yet enjoys
The shapes of this new world, in giant toys
Wrought by the busy   ever new?
Remembrance borrows Fancy's glass, to show
These forms more   sincere
Than now they are, than then, perhaps, they were.
When everything familiar seemed to be
Wonderful, and the immortality
Of this great world, which all things must inherit,
Was felt as one with the awakening spirit,
Unconscious of itself, and of the strange
Distinctions which in its proceeding change
It feels and knows, and mourns as if each were
A desolation.
            1821.

XXXV.

Were it not a sweet refuge, Emily,
For all those exiles from the dull insane
Who vex this pleasant world with pride and pain,
For all that band of sister-spirits known
To one another by a voiceless tone?
            1821.

XXXVI.

In one mode of considering those two classes of action of the human mind which are called reason and imagination, the former may be considered as mind employed upon the relations borne by one thought to another, however produced, and imagination as mind combining the elements of thought itself. It has been termed the power of association; and on an accurate anatomy of the functions of mind, it would be difficult to assign any other origin to the mass of what we perceive and know than this power. Association is, however, rather a law according to which this power is exerted than the power itself; in the same manner as gravitation is a passive expression of the reciprocal tendency of heavy bodies towards their respective centres. Were these bodies conscious of such a tendency, the name which they would assign to that consciousness would express the cause of gravitation; and it were a vain inquiry as to what might be the cause of that cause. Association bears the same relation to imagination as a mode to a source of action: when we look upon shapes in the fire or the clouds, and image to ourselves the resemblance of familiar objects, we do no more than seize the relation of certain points of visible objects, and fill up, blend together, * * * *

The imagination is a faculty not less imperial and essential to the happiness and dignity of the human being, than the reason.

It is by no means indisputable that what is true, or rather that which the disciples of a certain mechanical and superficial philosophy call true, is more excellent than the beautiful.

[These sentences seem to have formed part of the original exordium of the "Defence of Poetry," the composition of which was interrupted by an attack of ophthalmia.]

XXXVII.

Why is the reflection in that canal more beautiful than the objects it reflects? The colours are more vivid, and yet blended with more harmony; the openings from within into the soft and tender colours of the distant wood, and the intersection of the mountain lines, surpass and misrepresent truth.

1821.

XXXVIII.

The mountains sweep to the plain like waves that meet in a chasm—the olive woods are as green as a sea and are waving in the wind—the shadows of the clouds are spotting the bosoms of the hills—a heron comes sailing over me—a butterfly flits near—

at intervals the pines give forth their sweet and prolonged response to the wind—the myrtle bushes are in bud, and the soil beneath me is carpeted with odoriferous flowers.

1821.

XXXIX.

It is sweet to feel the beauties of nature in every pulsation, in every nerve—but it is far sweeter to be able to express this feeling to one who loves you. To feel all that is divine in the green-robed earth and the starry sky is a penetrating yet vivid pleasure which, when it is over, presses like the memory of misfortune; but if you can express those feelings—if, secure of sympathy (for without sympathy it is worse than the taste of those apples whose core is as bitter ashes), if thus secure you can pour forth into another's most attentive ear the feelings by which you are entranced, there is an exultation of spirit in the utterance—a glory of happiness which far transcends all human transports, and seems to invest the soul as the saints are with light, with a halo untainted, holy, and undying.

1821.

XL.

Bright wanderer, fair coquette of heaven,
To whom alone it has been given

To change and be adored for ever,
Envy not this dim world, for never
But once within its shadow grew
One fair as ———.

1822.

XLI.

    Even as my Master did,
Until Heaven's kingdom shall descend on earth,
Or earth be like a shadow in the light
Of heaven absorbed—some few tumultuous years
Will pass, and leave no wreck of what opposes
His will whose will is power.

1822.

[From "Charles I."]

ON THE TEXT OF SHELLEY'S POEMS.

NUMEROUS errors have crept into the text of Shelley's poems, especially such as were published when, from his absence on the Continent, he was unable to attend to the correction of the press,* and those posthumous pieces which were prepared for publication from almost illegible MSS. A careful inspection of the original whenever accessible has permitted the removal of many serious misprints, slight discrepancies between the MS. and the printed text are still more numerous, but as the former usually exists merely in the shape of notes, it would be unsafe to interfere with variations which would probably have been found in the copy as finally prepared for the press.

The emendations fall naturally into two classes—first,

---

* "In case you should accept the present offer, I will make one observation, which I consider of essential importance. It (*Valperga*) ought to be printed in half volumes at a time, and sent to the author for her last corrections by the post . . . Lord Byron has his works printed in this manner; and no person who has either fame to lose or money to win, ought to publish in any other."—*Shelley to Mr. Ollier;* "Memorials," p. 158.

those for which there is MS. authority; secondly, those which, the original not being extant, are sufficiently recommended by internal evidence. Some of both kinds had been already suggested by the Editor to the late Mr. Moxon—the corrections were made in the pocket-edition of the Minor Poems, but not in the collected works.

I.—LINES WRITTEN NEAR NAPLES.

Stanza 1, l. 4,
        The purple noon's transparent *light*,
                Read *might*.

Next line,
        The breath of the moist *air* is light,
                Read *earth*.
(A correction previously suggested by Mr. Wilmott.)

Ode to the West Wind.

Stanza 2, l. 11,
        The *doom* of a vast sepulchre,
                Read *dome*.

Stanza 4, l. 8,
        The skiey speed,
        Read *thy* skiey speed.

Letter to Maria Gisborne.

Vol. iii. p. 276, l. 13,*
        Which in those hearts which *most* remember me,
                Read *must*.

P. 279, at the bottom,
        With *least* in the middle,
                Read *lead*.

---

* Edition of 1839.

Vol. iii. p. 283,
>Yet will he stand
>* * * *
>The foremost, while rebuke *stands* pale and dumb,
>>Read *cowers* (avoiding the repetition).

Same page,
>He who sits obscure
>In the exceeding lustre and the pure
>Intense irradiation of a mind,
>Which with its own internal *lustre* blind,
>>Read *lightning*.

P. 285,
>A strain too learned for a shallow age,
>Too wise for selfish bigots, let his page,
>Which charms the chosen spirits of the *age*,
>Fold itself up for a serener *clime*,
>>For the second *age*, read *time*.

Witch of Atlas.

Stanza 8, l. 5,
>And *Driope* and Faunus followed quick,
>>Read *Dryope*.

Stanza 21, l. 2,
>And her thoughts were each a minister,
>>Read her *own* thoughts.

Stanza 48, l. 8,
>For Thamandocona, read Thamandoc*a*na.

Stanza 69, l. 4,
>For *thenceforth*, read *thenceforward*.

Line 7,
>Was a green and over-arching bower,
>>Read, was *as* a green, &c.

The Waning Moon.

Vol. iv. p. 41,
>The moon arose up *on* the murky *earth*,
>Read, The moon arose up *in* the murky *East*.

Motto to Epipsychidion.

L'anima amante si slancia *furio* del creato.   Read *fuori*.

P. 64, six lines from the bottom,
A tender
Reflection *on* the eternal moon of love,
Read *of*.

P. 72, l. 18,
In the *froze* air, read *frore*.

P. 73, l. 1,
Thin spheres of light, who rule this passive earth,
Read *twin*.

Lines to ———.   Vol. iv. p. 219,
And *from* all others, life and love,
Read *form*.

Fragment.   Vol. iv. p. 133, l. 15,
He faints, dissolved into a *sense* of love,
Read *sea*.

The Zucca.   Stanza 5, l. 6,
The *fresh grass* shown,
Transpose the words in italics.

Charles I., sc. 2, l. 20,
Scoffs at the *stake*,
Read *state*.

Fragment III., l. 3.
Which fairies catch in hyacinth *buds*,
Read *bowls*.

Scenes from Calderon, sc. 3.
Vol. iv. p. 329,
Twixt *thou* and me,
Read *thee*.

Vol. iv. p. 331,

> Thou melancholy thought, which art
> So *fluttering* and so sweet,

> Read *fluttering*.

Scenes from Faust, p. 352, l. 7,

> For *Felunsee*, read *Felsensee*.

II.—ALASTOR.

Vol. i. p. 132, l. 6.

> Islanded seas, blue mountains, mighty streams,
> Dim *tracks* and vast,

> Read *tracts*.

Revolt of Islam, canto I., stanza 49,

> 'Twas likest heaven, ere yet day's purple *streak*
> Ebbs o'er the western forest, while the gleam
> Of the unrisen moon,

> Read *stream*.

In the preface to this poem, Shelley speaks of a passage which he desires may be considered as an erratum, " where an alexandrine is most inadvertently left in the middle of a stanza:" the reference must be to Canto V. st. 44, where the text as hitherto printed has :—

> A form most like the imagined habitant
> Of silver exhalations *sprung* from dawn,
> By winds which feed on sunrise, *woven* to enchant
> The faiths of men.

Omit *woven* from the third line, and substitute it for *sprung* in the second.

"A Summer Evening Churchyard, *Lechdale*, Gloucestershire,"
Read *Lechlade*.

>*Marianne's Dream,* last stanza but one,
>>And through the chasm the *floor* did break,
>>With an earth-uplifting cataract,
>>>Read *flood.*

To a Skylark, st. 3. There can be no hesitation in admitting Professor Craik's most felicitous emendation, *embodied* for *unbodied,* nor in expunging the semicolon from the preceding stanza. Some other corrections proposed by him* had already been made in editions subsequent to 1839, others have been confirmed on examination of the MSS., and this would no doubt have been the case with many more had the pieces received the ultimate revision of the author.

>*To a lady with a Guitar,* last line,
>>For *our* beloved friend alone.

Mr. Palgrave is certainly right in proposing *one.* He ingeniously conjectures *viol* for *idol* in the couplet :—

---

* "History of English Literature," vol. ii., pp. 498-500. Professor Craik is only wrong in questioning the present reading of the initial couplet of "Epipsychidion" :—
>'Sweet spirit, sister of the orphan one,
>>Whose empire is the name thou weepest on.'

The meaning becomes clear on a little consideration. The orphan one, Emilia's spiritual sister, is Mary Shelley, whose mother died in giving her birth ; the name is Shelley's own.

> The artist who this *idol* wrought,
> To echo all harmonious thought.

But *idol* is used in the Platonic sense, and the guitar spoken of as the instrument by which the harmonious thought, otherwise abstract and impalpable to the senses, is *imaged* forth (εἰδωλον). *Sea-girt* for *sun-girt* in the "Lines among the Euganean Hills," is specious, but hardly to be adopted without MS. authority. It is unnecessary to discuss the merits of another of Mr. Palgrave's emendations, *locks* for *looks* in the lines from the "Prometheus Unbound:"

> Looks, where whoso gazes,
> Faints, entangled in their mazes,

since in an Italian prose translation made by Shelley himself the disputed word is rendered *sguardi*. What is meant by the mazes of looks appears from Asia's speech to Panthea in the second act:—

> Thy eyes are like the deep, blue, boundless heaven,
> Contracted to two circles underneath
> Their long fine lashes; dark, far, measureless,
> Orb within orb, and line through line inwoven.

In "Leigh Hunt's Correspondence," vol. ii. p. 266, is a letter from an illustrious living poet, giving some most interesting particulars respecting a MS. of "Lines to an Indian Air," found in Shelley's pocket after his death, and differing in several respects from the received version. Mr. Browning, however, seems to have been only able to refer to the text of the Posthumous Poems (1824): one of the variations has since been adopted; another, "O press it to thine own again," is certainly an improvement. Several fragmentary versions of the piece exist among Shelley's manuscripts, all differing more or less from the printed text and each other. According to Captain Medwin, the "Indian Air" was in reality a Persian one, but brought from India by Mrs. Williams.

LETTERS TO LEIGH HUNT.

[The following letters, with the exception of the fifth, were given to Sir Percy and Lady Shelley by Leigh Hunt, a few days before his death.]

SHELLEY TO LEIGH HUNT.

FLORENCE, *Nov.* 2, 1819.

MY DEAR FRIEND,

You cannot but know how sensibly I feel your kind expressions concerning me in the third part of your observations on the *Quarterly:* I feel that it is from a friend. As to the perverse-hearted writer of those calumnies, I feel assured that it is Southey,* and the only notice which it becomes me to take of it, is to seek an occasion of personal expostulation with him on my return to England—not on the ground, however, of what he has written in the *Review*, but on another ground. As to anonymous criticism, it is a much fitter subject for merriment than serious comment; except, indeed, when the latter can be made a vehicle, as you have done, of the kindest friendship.

Now, I only send you a *very heroic* poem,† which I wish you to give to Ollier, and desire him to print and

* This was an error.   † *Peter Bell the Third.*

publish immediately, you being kind enough to take upon yourself the correction of the press—not, however, with my name; and you must tell Ollier that the author is to be kept a secret, and that I confide in him for this object as I would confide in a physician or lawyer, or any other man whose professional situation renders the betraying of what is entrusted a dishonour. My motive in this is solely not to prejudge myself in the present moment, as I have only expended a few days in this party squib, and, of course, taken little pains. The verses and language I have let come as they would, and I am about to publish more serious things this winter; afterwards, that is next year, if the thing should be remembered so long, I have no objection to the author being known, but *not now*. I should like well enough that it should both go to press and be printed very quickly; as more serious things are on the eve of engaging both the public attention and mine.

Next post day you will hear from me again, as I have many things to say, and expect to have to announce Mary's *new work*, now in the press. She has written out, as you will observe, *my* Peter, and this is, I suspect, the last thing she will do before the new birth. Affectionately yours,

My dear Friend,

P. B. S.

[The "kind expressions concerning me in the third part of your observations on the *Quarterly*," were these :—

To return to Mr. Shelley. The Reviewer asserts that he "is shamefully dissolute in his conduct." We heard of similar assertions when we resided in the same house with Mr. Shelley for nearly three months; and how was he living all that time? As much like Plato himself, as all his theories resemble Plato— or rather, still more like a Pythagorean. This was the round of his daily life—he was up early; breakfasted sparingly; wrote this "Revolt of Islam" all the morning; went out in his boat, or into the woods with some Greek author or the Bible in his hands; came home to a dinner of vegetables (for he took neither meat nor wine); visited, if necessary, the sick and fatherless, whom others gave Bibles to and no help; wrote or studied again, or read to his wife and friends the whole evening; took a crust of bread, or a glass of whey for his supper; and went early to bed. This is literally the whole of the life he led, or that we believe he now leads in Italy; nor have we ever known him, in spite of the malignant and ludicrous exaggerations on this point, deviate, notwithstanding his theories, even into a single action which those who differ with him might think blameable. We do not say that he would always square his conduct by their opinions as a matter of principle; we only say that he acted just as if he did so square it. We forbear, out of regard for the very bloom of their beauty, to touch upon numberless other charities and generosities which we have known him exercise; but this we must say, in general, that we never lived with a man who gave so complete an idea of an ardent and principled aspirant in philosophy as Percy Shelley, and that we believe him, from the bottom of our hearts, to be one of the noblest hearts as well as heads which the world has seen for a long time. We never met, in short, with a being who came nearer, perhaps so near, to that height of humanity mentioned in the conclusion of an essay of Lord Bacon's, where he speaks of excess of charity, and of its not being in the power of "man or angel to come in danger by it."—*Examiner*, Oct. 10, 1819.]

SHELLEY TO LEIGH HUNT.

PISA, *March* 2, 1822.

MY DEAREST FRIEND,

My last two or three letters have, I fear, given you some uneasiness, or at least inflicted that portion of it which I felt in writing them. The aspect of affairs has somewhat changed since the date of that in which I expressed a repugnance to a continuance of intimacy with Lord Byron, so close as that which now exists; at least, it has changed so far as regards you and the intended journal. He expresses again the greatest eagerness to undertake it, and proceed with it, as well as the greatest confidence in you as his associate. He is for ever dilating upon his impatience of your delay, and his disappointment at your not having already arrived. He renews his expressions of disregard for the opinion of those who advised him against this alliance with you, and I imagine it will be no very difficult task to execute that which you have assigned me—to keep him in heart with the project until your arrival. Meanwhile, let my last letters, as far as they regard Lord Byron, be as if they had not been written. Particular circumstances, or rather, I should say, particular dispositions in Lord Byron's character, render the close and exclusive intimacy with him in which I find myself intolerable to me; thus much, my best friend, I will confess and confide to you. No feelings of my own shall injure or interfere with what is now nearest to them—your interest, and I will take care to preserve the little influence I may have over this Proteus in whom such strange extremes are reconciled, until we meet—which we now must, at all events, soon do. * * *

Lord Byron showed me your letter to him, which arrived with mine yesterday. How shall I thank you for your generous and delicate defence and explanation of my motives? I fear no misinterpretation from you, and from anyone else I despise and defy it.*

So you think I can make nothing of Charles the First. *Tanto peggio.* Indeed, I have written nothing for this last two months: a slight circumstance gave a new train to my ideas, and shattered the fragile edifice when half built. What motives have I to write? I *had* motives, and I thank the God of my own heart they were totally different from those of the other apes of humanity who make mouths in the glass of the time. But what are *those* motives now? The only inspiration

---

* In "Leigh Hunt's Correspondence," vol. ii., p. 180, is a fragment of a letter in which he questions the genuineness of a letter from Shelley to Byron, applying on his behalf and at his request for pecuniary assistance, and published in Moore's life of the latter. On subsequently finding the present letter among his papers, he became convinced of his mistake, and acknowledged it in a communication to Lady Shelley. He added, however, that he never received the loan of which Shelley obtained the promise; what circumstance may have intercepted it, cannot now be ascertained.

of an ordinary kind I could descend to acknowledge would be the earning £100 for you; and that it seems I cannot.

Poor Marianne, how ill she seems to have been! Give my best love to her, and tell her I hope she is better, and that I know as soon as she can resolve to set sail, that she will be better. Your rooms are still ready for you at Lord Byron's. I am afraid they will be rather hot in the summer; they were delightful winter rooms. My post [MS. illegible] must be transformed by your delay into a *paulo post futurum*.

Lord Byron begs me to ask you to send the enclosed letter to London in an enclosure, stating when you mean to sail, and in what ship. It is addressed to the wife of his valet Fletcher, who wishes to come out to join him under your protection, and, I need not tell you to promise her safety and comfort. * * * All happiness attend you, my best friend, and believe that I am watching over your interests with the vigilance of painful affection. Mary will write next post. Adieu.

Yours, S.

MRS. SHELLEY TO LEIGH HUNT.

Pisa, *April 27th*, 1822.

My dear Hunt,

*   *   *   *   *

You will wonder what the enclosed is. If you read the first page you will find it is an account of a brawl between five gentlemen, whose names are subjoined, and a soldier here. It made a great noise, for the man (as you will find by the first affidavit) was wounded by a pitchfork, and his life despaired of for some days. He was wounded, as he asserted, by a servant of Lord Byron's, and two of them are still imprisoned on suspicion, though we know that those two in particular are perfectly innocent.

The mode of conducting the judicial part of the affair is a specimen of their law here. While the man was in danger, not a single step was taken, and the man who wounded him had every opportunity to escape. As he got better they imprisoned these two men on suspicion, and they have been kept a fortnight on jail allowance, without being allowed to see any friend, not even their wives, or to receive any assistance, or even a change of linen from their friends.

*   *   *   *   *

Of course, if none of the public papers take notice of this affair, do you not in your "Examiner," for there is no great glory attached to such a row. If, however, any garbled accounts get current, I should think you might manufacture from these documents, which are the judicial ones, a true statement. I ought not to omit that a lady writes to me from Florence, to say, that she hears nothing but praise of Lord Byron's and his friends' conduct on this occasion, both from the English minister (Mr. Dawkins) and the Tuscan Court.

So much, my dear friend, for this business, to which Lord Byron attaches considerable importance, although to us, ever since the convalescence of the soldier, it has been a matter of perfect indifference. It appears to me a dream that you will ever reach these Tuscan shores—one begins to distrust everything after so many disappointments. You will find Shelley in infinitely better health; indeed he has got over this winter delightfully. Pisa is a paradise during that season for invalids, although I fear Marianne will find it rather hot in the summer; but once here, I doubt not but that in some way all will go well.

You do not mention your health in the last letter; but I do not doubt that it is improved in exact proportion to the number of miles you are distant from London. God knows when I shall again see that *benedetto luogo;* but even at this distance it sometimes strikes me with sudden fright, to think that any chain binds me to it.

My love to M. I hope to have no answer to this letter, but that you will in person acknowledge it.

My dear Hunt,

Affectionately yours,

Mary W. S.

SHELLEY TO LEIGH HUNT.

[AT GENOA.]

Lerici, *June* 19, 1822.

My Dearest Friend,

I write to you on the chance that you may not have left Genoa before my letter can reach you. Your letter was sent to Pisa, and thence forwarded here, or I should probably have ventured to meet you at Genoa; but the chances are now so much diminished of finding you, that I will not run the risk of the delay of seeing you that would be caused by our missing each other on the way. I shall therefore set off for Leghorn the moment that I hear you have sailed ———. We now inhabit a white house, with arches, near the town of Lerici, in the gulf of Spezzia. The Williamses are with us. Williams is one of the best fellows in the world; and Jane his wife a most delightful person, whom we all agree is the exact antitype of the lady I described in "The Sensitive Plant," though this must have been *a pure anticipated cognition*, as it was written a year before I knew her. I wish you need not pass Lerici, which I fear you will do; cast your eye on the white house, and think of us.

A thousand welcomes, my best friend, to this divine country; high mountains and seas no longer divide those whose affections are united. We have much to think of and talk of when we meet at Leghorn; but the final result of our plans will be peace to you, and to me a greater degree of consolation than has been permitted me since we met. My best love to Marianne, whose illness will soon disappear with the causes of it. If any circumstance *should* make you stop at Lerici, imagine the delightful surprise ———. Poor Mary, who sends you a thousand loves, has been seriously ill. She is still too unwell to rise from the sofa, and must take great care of herself for some time, or she would come with us to Leghorn. Lord Byron is in *villeggiatura*, near Leghorn; and you will meet besides with a Mr. Trelawny, a wild but kind-hearted seaman * *.

Give me the earliest intelligence of your motions.

LEIGH HUNT TO SHELLEY.

Shelley Mio,   Pisa, 9th July,* 1822.

Pray let us know how you got home the other day with Williams, for I fear you must have been out in the bad weather, and we are anxious. Things go on remarkably well.† Lord B. has given power to my brother John to get all his magazinable MSS. out of the hands of Murray. I am writing every morning; and the sooner we have your own MS. to send off, the better. Loves from Marianne and myself, which you must divide as becomes such precious commodity. When shall we see Marina and all of you? Marianne often wants you for the sublime purpose of facilitating her dialogues on shirts and neckcloths.   Yours affectionately,

L. H.

---

* The day after Shelley's death.

† In Shelley's last letter to Mrs. Shelley (Pisa, July, 4, 1822, lxviii. of the published correspondence) he says: "He [Byron] seems inclined to depart without the necessary explanations and arrangements due to such a situation as Hunt's. These, in spite of delicacy, I must procure. He offers him the copyright of the "Vision of Judgment" for the next number. This offer, if sincere, is more than enough to set up the journal; and if sincere, will set everything right." It would appear that everything had been satisfactorily arranged previous to Shelley's departure; and, but for his death, the differences between Byron and Hunt would probably never have occurred. Byron knew the value of a disinterested friend, and would have been very careful how he alienated the only person, the Countess Guiccioli excepted, whom he could consider in that light.

FROM A LETTER FROM MRS. SHELLEY TO LEIGH HUNT.

Concluded at Susa, *July* 28, 1823.

I was too late for the post yesterday at Turin, and too early this morning; so, as I determined to put this letter in the post myself, I bring it with me to Susa, and now open it to tell you how delighted I am with my morning's ride—the scenery is so divine. The high dark Alps, just on this southern side tipt with snow, close in a plain; the meadows are full of clover and flowers, and the woods of ash, elm, and beech, descend and spread and lose themselves in the fields; stately trees in clumps or singly arise on each side, and wherever you look you see some spot where you dream of building a house and living for ever. The exquisite beauty of nature, and the cloudless sky of this summer day, soothe me, and make this 28th so full of recollections as to be almost pleasurable.* Wherever the spirit of beauty dwells, he must be. The rustling of the trees is full of him—the waving of the tall grass—the moving shadows of the vast hills—the blue air that penetrates their ravines, and rests upon their heights. I feel him near me when I see that which he best loved; alas, nine years ago he took to a home in his

* It was the anniversary of Shelley's and Mary's departure for the Continent in 1814.

heart this weak being, whom he has now left for more congenial spirits and happier regions. She lives only in the hope that she may become one day as one of them.

Absolutely, my dear Hunt, I will pass some three summer months in this divine spot—you shall all be with me. There are no gentlemen's seats or palazzi, so we will take a cottage, which we will paint and refit, just as this country inn is in which I now write—clean and plain. We will have no servants; only we will give out all the needlework. Marianne shall make puddings and pies, to make up for the vegetables and meat which I shall boil and spoil. Thorny shall sweep the rooms, Mary make the beds, Johnny clean the kettles and pans, and then we will pop him into one of the many streams hereabouts, and so clean him. Swinny being so quick shall be our Mercury, Percy our gardener, Sylvan and Percy Florence our weeders, and Vincent our plaything; and then to raise us above the vulgar, we will do all our work keeping time to Hunt's symphonies; we will perform our sweepings and dustings to the march in Alceste; * we will [go to our m]eals to the tune of the laughing trio; and when we [are fatigued] we will lie on our turf sofas,

---

* " Scrubbing requires for true grace but frank and artistical handling,
   And the removal of slops to be ornamentally treated."
—*The Bothie of Toper-na-fuosich.*

while all [who have] voices shall [join in] chorus in "Notte e giorno faticar." You see [that my pap]er is quite out, so I must say, for the last time, adieu. God bless you.

MARY W. S.

Sunday, LYONS, *August 3rd*.

MY DEAR HUNT,

I arrived at Lyons yesterday evening, and remain here until Tuesday evening; this repose will, I trust, entirely restore Percy, and will give me time, I hope, to receive your letter, which is not yet arrived. I have taken my place in a public conveyance—not the diligence. I shall travel all Tuesday night and the day of Wednesday, and then repose a night and a day at Dijon, then again a night and a day of travelling, the same of repose, and Sunday afternoon I arrive at Paris. This I dare say will appear to you a queer mode of proceeding, but it was the best I could manage. I could not think of travelling three successive days and nights. Vetturino travelling is detestable from the slowness of the motion, and posting would be too expensive; but in this mode I unite cheapness, swiftness, and repose.

I have sent you a "Juvenal" by my vetturino who brought me here, and now returns to Italy. I sought for English books, but could find none, so I only send a "Paul and Virginia" for Thornton. I send you, also, the music of the "Clemenza di Tito;" it cost only seventeen francs, so I was tempted. I went to the music shop to buy some for you, but my ignorance both of what I ought to buy, and what you have, so puzzled me, that I was glad to settle on safe ground in buying Mozart; remembering my Polly's preference, I tried to get some of Handel, but there was none. You have "Ah perdona," but I do not think that you have "Deh prendi un dolce amplesso." And, besides, there must be many other things in an opera of Mozart. By the bye, send me a list of what music you would like to have, and what you have, that if I see any cheap I may know what I am about; and tell me also the name of that air of Handel's of which you are so fond. I do not mean, "He was despised and rejected of men," but the other of which you know only a few notes.

Have you received my two letters, one *impostata* at Susa, the other at Pont Bon-voisin? They will have shown you how I got on during the first days. I look back with surprise to the tranquillity I was able to preserve at that time; but this is to be attributed to your kindness, my dear friend, for the idea of leaving affectionate hearts behind me still preserves in an outward and visible form the bond which must ever exist between me and Italy. And now I turn southwards and ask, What are you doing? If you are not a rebel against all your own diaphragmatic theories, you are taking a long walk this fine evening. And you, Marianne—have you not been out?

From the quay here that overlooks the Rhone, we see Mont Blanc. This mountain is associated to me with many delightful hours: we lived under its eye at Geneva; and when at Lyons we looked with joy at its sublime dome. It is in itself so magnificent. The utmost heights of Cenis and the [MS. illegible] were only flecked with snow; Mont Blanc has still on its huge mantle, and its *aiguilles*, purer than the whitest marble, pierce the heaven around it. The sight of this might have given Michael Angelo a still finer idea of a " dome in the air " than the Pantheon itself.

I wonder, my best friend, if in other planets and systems there are other sublimer objects, and more lovely scenes, to entrance Shelley with still greater delight than he felt, at seeing these wondrous piles of earth's primæval matter; or does he only feel and see the beauties we contemplate with greater intensity? I fear that if he could send us any of his poetry from where he now is, the world would find it more unintelligible and elementary than that which we have. He loved nature so enthusiastically, that one is irresistibly led to imagine his painless spirit among its divinest combinations. In the society even of those he loved, I do not feel his presence so vividly as I do when I hear the wind among the trees—when I see the shadows on the mountains, the sunshine in the ravines, or behold heaven and earth meet when she arises towards it, or the clouds descend to her. During the winter, how horrible was the sound and look of the sea; but I began to love it, and fancy him near it when it sparkled beneath the sun; yet after all, dear Hunt, I was surprised to find that I felt his presence more vividly during my journey through the ravines of the Alps, near the roar of the waterfalls, and the "inland murmur" of the precipitous rivers. How I should delight to make a tour with you among these scenes; feeling him and all about him, as you do, still you would know him better if you visited these spots, which he loved better than any others in the world.

Tuesday, August 5th.

I have your letter, and your excuses and all. I thank you most sincerely for it. At the same time, I do entreat you to take care of yourself with regard to writing, although your letters are worth infinite pleasure to me; yet that pleasure cannot be worth pain to you. And remember, if you must write, the good hacknied maxim of *multum in parvo*, and when your temples throb, distil the essence of three pages into three lines, and my "fictitious adventure"* will enable me to open them out and fill up intervals; not but what three pages are best—but "you understand me." And now let me tell you that I fear you do not rise early, since you doubt my "*ore mattutine.*" Be it known to you, then, that on the journey I always rose *before* three o'clock, that I *never* once made the vetturino wait; and, moreover, that there was no discontent in our jogging on, on either side, so that I half expect to be a *santa* with him. He, indeed, got a little out of his element when he got into France; his good humour did not leave him, but his self-possession. He could not speak French, and he walked about as if treading on eggs.

When at Paris I will tell you more what I think of the French. They still seem miracles of quietness in comparison with Marianne's noisy friends; and the women's dresses afford the drollest contrast with those in fashion when I first set foot in Paris in 1814. Then their waists were between their shoulders, and, as Hogg observed, they were rather curtains than gowns. Their hair, too, dragged to the top of the head, and then lifted to its height, appeared as if each female wished to be a Tower of Babel in herself. Now their

---

* Alluding to an expression in a letter from Godwin: "Your talents, as far as I can at present discern, are turned for the writing of fictitions adventures."—*Shelley Memorials,* p. 218.

waists are long (not so long, however, as the Genoese), and their hair flat at the top, with quantities of curls on the temples. I remember in 1814 a Frenchman's pathetic horror at my appearance in the streets of Paris in Oldenburgh (as they were called) hats: now they all wear machines of that shape, and a high bonnet would of course be as far out of the right road, as if the earth were to take a flying leap to another system.

After you receive this letter, you must direct to me to my father's (pray put " W. G., Esq.," since the want of that etiquette annoys him. I remember Shelley's unspeakable astonishment when the author of "Political Justice" asked him, half reproachfully, why he addressed him as "Mr. G."*), 195, Strand; and since the 21st is the day, I suppose I ought to write to Florence. However, when in Paris, I will calculate the time and direct accordingly. Remember, Via del Fonda. I will send you the number of the house from Paris; I think it was called Palazzo Morano, or Morandi, but the number will settle that.

* "In speaking of him to his own original, peculiar friends and associates, I have at first said 'Mr. Godwin,' but I was instantly corrected—I may perhaps say snubbed—by the emendation, 'William Godwin, you mean.' It was much as if I had spoken of a Quaker to Quakers, and adopted, to their discomfiture, terms implying creature-worship."—*Hogg's Life of Shelley*, vol. ii., p. 331.

Well, my dear Hunt, I must not clack any more, or Marianne will think me as bad as Manin,* except that you can silence me by not reading me. I hope you have taken measures that Mrs. Mason shall have "Valperga," as you write a criticism of it. If ever I write another novel, it will be better worth your criticism and more pleasing to you than this. After all, "Valperga" is merely a book of promise; another landing-place in the staircase I am climbing. I often think of "Alfred of Triamond." You must send me the list of books I must consult for it.

I hope Marianne thinks of me with kindness, and that the children remember me. Percy was playing at playing with Henry all day yesterday, and generously gave the shadow all his playthings. How are Polly's nerves, and the bell, and the empty house, and how goes on the jacket? *The* jacket, with the definite article. Has Henry yet profaned it with fruit-soiled hands? God bless you all, and bless you, dear Hunt, for all the good you have done me, do me, and are about to do. Faithfully yours,

MARY W. SHELLEY.

* I cannot explain this allusion.

MRS. SHELLEY TO LEIGH HUNT.

LONDON, *September 9th*, 1823.

MY DEAR HUNT,

Bessy promised me to relieve you from any inquietude you might suffer from not hearing from me, so I indulged myself with not writing to you until I was quietly settled in lodgings of my own. Want of time is not my excuse; I had plenty, but until I saw all quiet around me, I had not the spirit to write a line. I thought of you all—how much!—and often longed to write, yet would not till I called myself free to turn southward;—to imagine you all, to put myself in the midst of you, would have destroyed all my philosophy. But now I do so. I am in little neat lodgings, my boy in bed, I quiet, and I will now talk to you; tell you what I have seen and heard, and, with as little repining as I can, try (by making the best of what I have, the certainty of your friendship and kindness) to rest half content that I am not in the "Paradise of Exiles." * Well, first I will tell you, journalwise, the history of my sixteen days in London. I arrived Monday, the 25th of August. My father and William came for me to the wharf. I had an excellent passage of $11\frac{1}{2}$ hours, a glassy sea, and a contrary wind—the smoke of our fire was wafted right aft, and streamed out behind us; but the

* A phrase applied to Italy in *Julian and Maddalo*.

wind was of little consequence, the tide was with us; and though the engine gave a " short, uneasy motion " to the vessel, the water was so smooth that no one on board was sick, and Persino played about the deck in high glee. I had a very kind reception in the Strand, and all was done that could be done to make me comfortable. I exerted myself to keep up my spirits. The house, though rather dismal, is infinitely better than the Skinner Street one. I resolved not to think of certain things, to take all as a matter of course, and thus contrived to keep myself out of the gulf of melancholy, over the edge of which I was and am continually peeping.

But lo and behold! I found myself famous. " Frankenstein " had had prodigious success as a drama, and was about to be repeated for the 23rd night at the English Opera House. The play-bill amused me extremely, for in the list of *dramatis personæ* came ———, by Mr. T. Cooke; this nameless mode of naming the unnameable is rather good. On Friday, August 29th, Jane, my father, William, and I, went to the theatre to see it. Wallack looked very well as F. He is at the beginning full of hope and expectation. At the end of the first act the stage represents a room with a staircase leading to F.'s workshop; he goes to it, and you see his light at a small window, through which a frightened servant peeps, who runs off in terror, when

F. exclaims, "It lives!" Presently F. himself rushes in horror and trepidation from the room, and while still expressing his agony and terror, —— throws down the door of the laboratory, leaps the staircase, and presents his unearthly and monstrous person on the stage. The story is not well managed, but Cooke played ——'s part extremely well: his seeking, as it were, for support—his trying to grasp at the sounds he heard—all, indeed, he does, was well imagined and executed. I was much amused, and it appeared to excite a breathless eagerness in the audience. It was a third piece; a scanty pit filled at half-price, and all stayed till it was over. They continue to play it even now.

On Saturday, August the 30th, I went with Jane to the Gisbornes'. I know not why, but seeing them seemed more than anything else to remind me of Italy. Evening came on drearily. The rain splashed on the pavement, nor star nor moon deigned to appear. I looked upward, to seek an image of Italy, but a blotted sky told me only of my change. I tried to collect my thoughts, and then again dared not think, for I am a ruin where owls and bats live only, and I lost my last *singing bird* when I left Albaro. It was my birthday, and it pleased me to tell the people so—to recollect and feel that time flies; and what is to arrive is nearer, and my home not so far off as it was a year ago. This same evening, on my return to the Strand, I saw Lamb, who was very entertaining and amiable, though a little deaf. One of the first questions he asked me was, whether they made puns in Italy. I said, " Yes, now Hunt is there." He said that Burney made a pun in Otaheite, the first that was ever made in that country; at first the natives could not make out what he meant, but all at once they discovered the *pun*, and danced round him in transports of joy. L. said one thing, which I am sure will give you pleasure. He corrected for Hazlitt a new edition of " Elegant Extracts," in which living poets are included. He said he was much pleased with many of your things, with a little of Montgomery and a little of Crabbe. Scott he found tiresome. Byron had many fine things, but was tiresome; but yours appeared to him the freshest and best of all. These " Extracts " have never been published; they have been offered to Mr. Hunter; and seeing the book at his house, I had the curiosity to look at what the extracts were that pleased L. There was the canto of the Fatal Passion from " Rimini," several things from " Foliage," and from the " Amyntas." L. mentioned also your " Conversation with Coleridge," and was much pleased with it. He was very gracious to me, and invited me to see him when Miss L. should be well. * * *

Having secured neat cheap lodgings, I removed hither last night. Such, dear Hunt, is the outline of your poor Exile's history. After two days of rain, the weather has been *uncommonly* fine, *cioè* without rain, and cloudless, I believe; though I trust to other eyes for that fact, since the whitewashed sky is anything but blue to any but the perceptions of the natives themselves. It is so cold, however, that the fire I am now sitting by is not the first that has been lighted, for my father had one two days ago.

The wind is east and piercing, but I comfort myself with the hope that softer gales are now fanning your *not* throbbing temples—that the climate of Florence will prove kindly to you, and that your health and spirits will return to you. Why am I not there? This is quite a foreign country to me; the names of the places sound strangely; the voices of the people are new and grating—the vulgar English they speak particularly displeasing. But for my father, I should be with you next spring; but his heart and soul are set on my stay; and in this world it always seems one's duty to sacrifice one's own desires, and that claim ever appears the strongest which claims such a sacrifice.

On Tuesday, Sept. 2nd, I dined with Mr. Hunter and Bessy, and she afterwards drank tea with me at the Strand.

One thing at Mr. Hunter's amused me very much. Your piping Faun and kneeling Venus are on the piano; but from a feeling of delicacy they are turned with their backs to the company. I think of going down to Richmond on Friday, and taking a last peep at green fields and leaves before I return to my winter cage.

MRS. SHELLEY TO MRS. HUNT.

Nov. 27th [1823], LONDON.

MY DEAREST POLLY,

Are you not a naughty girl? How could you copy a letter to that " agreeable unaffected woman Mrs. Shelley," without saying a word from yourself to your loving grandmother? My dear Polly, a line from you forms a better picture for me of what you are all about than—alas! I was going to say three pages, but I check myself—than the rare one page of Hunt. Do not think that I forget you—even Percy does not, and he often tells me to bid the Signor Enrico and you to get in a carriage and then into a boat and to come to *questo paese* with baby *nuovo*, Henry, Swinburne *e tutti*. But that will not be: nor shall I see you at Mariano. This is a dreary exile for me: during a long month of cloud and fog how often have I sighed for my beloved Italy! Yet, in truth, as far as regards mere money matters and worldly prospects, I keep up my philosophy with excellent success: others wonder at this, but I do not; nor is there any philosophy in it. After having witnessed the mortal agonies of my two darling children— after that journey from and to Lerici, I feel all these as pictures and trifles as long as I am kept out of contact with the unholy. I was upset to-day by being obliged to see ⸺, and the prospect of seeing others of his tribe. I can earn a sufficiency, I doubt not. In Italy I should be content. Here I will not bemoan—indeed I never do; and Mrs. ⸺ makes *large eyes* at the quiet way in which I take it all. It is England alone that annoys me; yet sometimes I get among friends, and almost forget its fogs. I go to Shacklewell rarely, and sometimes see the Novellos elsewhere. He is my especial favourite, and his music always transports me to the seventh heaven.

I see the Lambs rather often: she ever amiable, and Lamb witty and delightful. I must tell you one thing, and make H. laugh. Lamb's new house, at Islington, is close to the New River, and George Dyer, after having paid them a visit, on going away at twelve at noonday, walked deliberately into the water, taking it for the high road. But, as he said afterwards to Procter, "I soon found that I was in the water, sir." So Miss L. and the servant had to fish him out. I must tell Hunt, also, a good saying of Lamb's: talking of some one, he said, "Now some men who are very veracious are called matter-of-fact men; but such an one I should call a matter-of-lie man."

I have seen, also, Procter, with his "beautifully formed head" (it *is* beautifully formed) several times, and I like him. He is an enthusiastic admirer of Shelley, and most zealous in the bringing out the volume of his poems;* this alone would please me, and he is moreover gentle and gentlemanly, and apparently endued with a true poetic feeling. Besides, he is an invalid; and some time ago I told you in a letter that I have always a sneaking (for sneaking, read open) kindness for men of literary, and particularly poetic, habits who have delicate health. I cannot help revering the mind delicately attuned, that shatters the material frame, and whose thoughts are strong enough to throw down and dilapidate the walls of sense and dikes of flesh that the unimaginative contrive to keep in such good repair. * * * Peacock says Hogg is grown thinner; and I suppose he is, since he is not, as you described him, fat, but is the same in person and everything (*una cosa di meno*), as far as I can see, and his colour, which often changes, shows, I think, that his sensibility remains. * * *

After all I spend a great deal of my time in solitude.

* The expenses of publication were, in fact, guaranteed by Mr. Procter and two generous associates. One of these was, I believe, T. F. Kelsall, Esq., the other was the late T. L. Beddoes, author of "Death's Jest-Book"—a poet far too truly poetical for the general taste, but who in point of imaginative intensity approached more nearly to Shelley than any other of his contemporaries, Keats only excepted.

I have been hitherto fully occupied in preparing Shelley's MSS. It is now complete, and the poetry alone will make a large volume. Will you tell Hunt that he need not send any of the MSS. that he has (except the "Essay on Devils,"* and some lines addressed to himself on his arrival in Italy, if he should choose them to be inserted), as I have recopied all the rest. We should be very glad, however, of his notice as quickly as possible, as we wish the book to be out in a month at furthest, and that will not be possible unless he sends it immediately; it would break my heart if the book should appear without it.† When he does send a packet over (let it be directed to his brother), will he also be so good as to send me a copy of my "Choice," ‡ beginning after the line "Entrenched sad lines, or blotted with its might." Perhaps, dear Marianne, you would have the kindness to copy them for me, and send them soon. I have another favour to ask of you. Miss Curran has a portrait of Shelley, in many things very like, and she has so much talent that I entertain great hopes that she will be able to make a good one;

---

* This amusing fragment was prepared for publication in 1839, with the rest of Shelley's prose works, but withdrawn, for reasons which seven other essayists have since conspired to deprive of much of their weight. The lines addressed to Leigh Hunt have unfortunately been lost.

† It did, however.

‡ A poem by Mrs. Shelley, thus entitled.

for this purpose I wish her to have all the aids possible, and among the rest a profile from you.* If you could not cut another, perhaps you would send her one already cut; and if you sent it with a note requesting her to return it when she had done with it, I will engage that it will be most faith[fully returned]. At present I am not quite sure where she is, but I [MS. illegible] should be there, and you can find her and send her this. I need not tell you how you would oblige me; you would oblige Henry† if he got a good portrait.

I have heard from Bessy that Hunt is writing something for the *Examiner* for me. I conjecture that this may be concerning "Valperga." I shall be glad indeed when that comes, or, in lieu of it, anything else. John Hunt begins to despair, since he says that without Indicators the L[iterary] E[xaminer] must fail. That the *E.* is so constituted now, on account of the admission

---

* Mrs. Hunt—no mean proficient in much higher walks of art—was renowned for her cleverness in cutting out profiles in paper or cardboard. The frontispiece to "Lord Byron and his Contemporaries" is an example.

† The son of Leigh Hunt's brother John, and one of the publishers of the "Liberal" and Shelley's posthumous poems. The portrait did not arrive till long afterwards. Beddoes says, in a letter to Mr. Procter (Milan, June 9, 1824): "If I could be any use in bringing the portrait, &c., it would be a proud task, but most likely I only flash over Florence; entering in the flood of the stars, and departing with their ebb." (Memoir prefixed to his works, p. xxxv.)

of advertisements, that anything not immediately of the day could not be printed in it, and that he despairs of the possibility of setting up anything new.

And now, dear Polly, I think I have done with gossip and business — with words of affection and kindness I should never have done. I am inexpressibly anxious about you all. Percy has had a similar, though shorter, attack to that at Albaro, but he is now recovered. I have a cold in my head, occasioned, I suppose, by the weather. Ah, Polly! if the beauties of England were to have only the mirror that Richard III. desires, a very short time would be spent at the looking-glass. What of Florence and the gallery? I saw the Elgin marbles to-day—to-morrow I am to go to the Museum and look over the prints; that will be a great treat. The Theseus is a divinity. But how very few statues they have! Kiss the children. Ask Thornton for his promised and forgotten P. S. Give my love to Hunt, and believe me, my dear Marianne, the exiled but ever most

Affectionately yours,
Mary W. S.

MRS. SHELLEY TO LEIGH HUNT.

5, Bartholmoew Place, Kentish Town,
July 29*th*, [1824].

I hope, my dear Hunt, that you will receive the volume of Shelley's poems, which I have sent you through Mrs. Mason. It is, I believe, selling tolerably well. Since writing to Marianne, I have removed to this part of the world; but this, I may say, is the only change that has taken place in my situation, except, indeed, that alteration in spirit which is occasioned by a miraculous duration of fine weather. We (*i.e.* the English—I used to say *they, aimè!* talking of the natives) have not had such a summer, they say, for these five years; *manca* a shower or two, we have not had a mizzle this fortnight. They call it hot—it is not—but it is pleasant weather; a little cloudy or so, but so convenient in heat, that I echo an Italian image-seller, who said to me, " Sarei contento se durasse."

I had a letter the other day from Trelawny; it was dated Missolonghi, to which place he had come hoping to save or attend on the last moments of Lord Byron, but he came too late. The funeral, last week, passed my home. What should I have said to a Cassandra, who three years ago should have prophesied that Jane and I—Edward and Shelley gone—should watch the funereal procession of Lord Byron up Highgate Hill? All changes of romance or drama lag far behind this. Trelawny is sanguine about the cause and his own personal advancement. He has formed a friendship also for a young man (I suppose a Greek), whom he compares to Shelley in enthusiasm and talent.

* * * * *

I lead a very different life now from that which I did during the winter—something that approaches to my Italian one. Jane and I live near each other, and see each other almost every day; we dwell on the past and dream of future Italy. I make hardly any visits except to my father, and endeavour to be as recluse as I can, without giving up the friendship of the very few who are dear to me. Operas and theatres are over for me now in summer-time.

I long to hear from you. I fear that you are not well or happy, and this long silence on your part seems to arise from that. I wish we could change places. I should not wish for better than the chesnut-covered hills and olive groves of Maiano; glowing sunsets, fire-flies, the cry of the aziola, the language of the [MS. illegible] Toscano—things associated to me with my happiest days; you would be pleased with a quiet abode in Kentish Town—a stroll through its green meadows, and rambles up its gentle hills—very pretty things, no doubt; and I make the best of them, delighted to have escaped dreary London, and resolved to enjoy the summer.

Mr. Beddoes (a very great admirer of our Shelley *) is now in Italy. He is to get the portrait from Miss Curran, who I fancy is in Rome. Could not Marianne send one of the profiles already cut to Miss Curran (who I know would return it with care), and who by this means would make a better likeness than any that exists at present? I own that my heart is set upon Marianne's doing this; for what would I not give for a portrait which, while he was with me, I so often resolved to obtain, and was obliged perpetually to disappoint myself? Marianne wished for scissors, which I had no opportunity of sending, but she has some cut. Give my love to her, and tell her I throw myself at her feet, and implore her to comply with my request.

---

* Shelley's book! This is a ghost indeed, and one who will answer to our demand for hidden treasure. The "Dirge for the Year"—that Indian fragment, "The Boat on the Serchio"—and "The Letter," with "Music," are to me the best of the new things, and perfectly worthy of the mind which produced them . . . What would he not have done, if ten years more that will be wasted on the lives of unprofitable knaves and fools, had been given to him! Was it that more of the beautiful and good than Nature could spare to one was incarnate in him, and that it was necessary to resume it for distribution through the internal and external worlds? How many springs will blossom with his thoughts! how many fair and glorious creations be born of his one extinction!—*Memoir of T. L. Beddoes*, p. xxxvi.

How is she, poor thing? and how is Thorny and dear Henry, whom Percy has not forgotten.

It would give me great pleasure if either you or Marianne would write. I love you both tenderly. I am ever,

Your affectionate
MARY W. SHELLEY.

MRS. SHELLEY TO LEIGH HUNT.

KENTISH TOWN, *Aug.* 22, [1824].

MY DEAR HUNT,

ALTHOUGH I know that you wish yourself in England, yet it seems to me as if I wrote to Paradise from Purgatory. Our summer is over, and rain and perpetual cloud veil this dreary land. I wish you were here, since you wish it; yet from all I hear, the period does not seem near. Poor dear Marianne, she goes on suffering; and God knows what would become of her in this ungenial climate. Jane and I dream and talk only of our return; and I begin to think that next autumn this may be possible. I have been obliged, however, as an indispensable preliminary, to suppress the posthumous poems. More than 300 copies had been sold, so this is the less provoking; and I have been obliged to promise not to bring dear Shelley's name before the public again during Sir T.'s life. There is no great harm in this, since from choice I should not think of writing memoirs now, and the materials for a volume of more works are so scant that I doubted before whether I could publish it. All this was pending when I wrote last, but until I was certain, I did not think it worth while to mention it. The affair is arranged by Peacock, who, though I seldom see him, seems anxious to do me all these kind of services in the best manner that he can.

Poor Pietro [Gamba] is now in London. "Non fosse male questo paese," he says, "se si vedesse mai il sole." He is full of Greece, to which he is going to return, and gave us an account of our good friend Trelawny, which shows that he is not at all changed. Trelawny has made a hero of the Greek chief Ulysses,* and declares that there is a great cavern in Attica which he and Ulysses have provisioned for seven years, and to which if the cause fails, he and this chieftain are to retire; but if the cause is triumphant, he is to build a city in the Negropont, colonise it, and Jane and I are to go out to be queens and chieftainesses of the Island. He has quarrelled very violently with Mavrocordato; but I easily divine how all this is. Poor Mavrocordato, beset by covetous Suliotes, disliked by the chieftains of the Morea, caballed against by the strangers, poor while every other chief is getting rich,

* Odysseus.

is drinking deep of the bitter cup of calumny and disappointment.

But to quit Greece and return to England. The Opera-house is closed. Before it shut, I heard Pasta, and never was more affected by any scenic representation, than by her acting of Romeo. She joins intellectual beauty, grace, perfect tragic action to a fine voice and a sentiment in singing I never saw equalled. When she sees *Giulietta* in the tomb—when she takes poison—when *Giulietta* awakes and her joy at meeting is changed to the throes of death—the whole theatre was in one transport of emotion. The novelty now is the "Freischutz" of Weber, performing at the Lyceum, and the music is wild but often beautiful. When the magic bullets are cast they fill the stage with all sorts of horrors—owls flapping their wings, toads crawling about, fiery serpents darting [MS. illegible], ghostly hunting in the clouds, while every now and then, in the midst of a stream of wild harmony, comes a crashing discord—all form, I assure you, a very fine scene, while every part of the house except the stage is enveloped in darkness.

One of my principal reasons for writing just now is that I have just heard Miss Curran's address (64, Via Sistina, Roma), and I am anxious that Marianne should, if she will be so very good, send one of the profiles already cut to her, of Shelley; since I think that by the help of that Miss Curran will be able to correct her portrait of Shelley, and make for us what we so much desire, a good likeness. I am convinced that Miss Curran will return the profile immediately that she has done with it—so that you will not sacrifice it, though you may be the means of our obtaining a good likeness. I will write soon to Marianne. In the mean time, I wish she would write to me, since I long to hear from her and should be very glad whenever you will be kind enough to assure me of the continuance of your friendship, although I fear it is gone to the "tomb of the Capulets." But I do not deserve this catastrophe. Give my love to your children—Occhi Turchini* among the rest—and believe me ever, my dear Hunt,

Your faithful friend,
Mary W. Shelley.

MRS. SHELLEY TO MRS. LEIGH HUNT.

Firenze.

Kentish Town, *Oct. 10th*, [1824].

My dearest Marianne,

My interest in you and your dear circle has been excited in the most lively and painful way by the news I have had of you through Bessy. One's first thought

---

* *Blue Eyes.*

is, can one not in any way aid these beloved exiles?—and then I shrink into myself in despair at my nothingness. If it were not for your's and Hunt's health, I am convinced that Novello's active friendship would dissipate other difficulties and restore you to the England you love. In the mean time are there not resources by which you might be rendered more comfortable where you are. J. H. says that Colburn wishes Hunt to contribute to the *New Monthly*. If this be true he would pay liberally, and Hunt need not feel delicacy towards his brother, since the latter has no violent wish that the "W. C.'s" should be continued. From what J. H. said, perhaps there is a negotiation with Colburn already on foot; if not, I can through Horace Smith (who is now in England, and expected daily in London), or in my own person, contribute to such an arrangement. I pray you employ me. I am anxious beyond measure to hear from you—from you, my Polly, in particular—since you will send me the most vivid picture of what is passing near. Write, if you love me.

I write to you on the most dismal of all days—a rainy Sunday; when dreary church-going faces look still more drearily from under dripping umbrellas, and the poor plebeian dame looks reproachfully at her splashed white stockings—not her gown, that has warily been held high up, and the to-be-concealed petticoat has borne all the ill-usage of the mud—dismal though it is, dismal though I am, I do not wish to write a discontented letter, but in a few words to describe things as they are with me. A weekly visit to the Strand, a monthly visit to Shacklewell (when we are sure to be caught in the rain), forms my catalogue of visits. The eternal rain imprisons one in one's little room, and one's spirits flag without one exhilarating circumstance. I read, study, and write—sometimes that takes me out of myself, but to live for no one, to be necessary to none; to know that—" where is now my hope? for my hope, who shall see it? they shall go down to the bars of the pit, when our rest together is in the dust." But change of scene to the sun of Italy will restore my energy. The very thought of it smooths my brow. Perhaps, never content with the climate, I shall seek the heats of Naples, if they do not hurt my darling Percy.

We had a fright the other day, fearing that Miss L[amb] was going to be taken ill, but she is now quite well—so she will escape this year. I was to have dined there to-day had it not been for the rain. She always asks most affectionately after you. Procter is married. The same paper that announced his marriage gave out the death of Lord C. Murray. I liked his letter to Hunt; I liked the feeling and the conduct of the man—and he is gone. Pietro Gamba is in town;

I have seen him often, I talk over old times. Peacock transacts my business with Sir T. S.'s solicitor, else I never see him. Coulson went to France last spring, and has not yet recovered from the enthusiasm inspired by the French woman and Notre Dame. Hazlitt is abroad; he will be in Italy in the winter. He wrote an article in the *Edinburgh Review* on the volume of poems which I published. I do not know whether he meant it to be favourable or not—I did not like it at all;* but when I saw him I could not be angry; I never was so shocked in my life—he is so changed and thin, his hair scattered, his cheek-bones projecting—but for his voice and smile I should not have known him. His smile brought tears into my eyes—it was like a sun-beam illuminating the most melancholy of ruins—lightning that assured you in a dark night of the identity of a friend's ruined and deserted abode. *

❃ ❃ ❃ ❃ ❃

Have you, my Polly, sent a profile to Miss C., in Rome? Now pray do, and pray write; do, my dear girl.

Percy is quite well. Tell his friend he goes to school and learns to read and write, being very handy

---

* It commences: "Mr. Shelley's style is to poetry what astrology is to natural science," and the note thus struck is kept up throughout. This unsatisfactory paper is, however, distinguished by all its author's wonted splendour of diction and imagery.

with his hands—perhaps having a pure anticipated cognition of the art of painting in his tiny fingers.

Have you heard of Medwin's book—notes of conversations that he had at Pisa with Lord Byron? Every one is to be in it; every one will be angry. He wanted me to have a hand in it, but I declined. Years ago, when a man died the worms ate him; now a set of worms feed on the carcase of the scandal that he leaves behind him, and grow fat upon the world's love of little talk—I will not be numbered among them. Adieu.

Yours affectionately,

MARY W. SHELLEY.

SHELLEY, HARRIET SHELLEY, AND MR. T. L. PEACOCK.

> Words
> That make a man feel strong in speaking truth.
> TENNYSON.

SHELLEY, HARRIET SHELLEY, AND MR. T. L. PEACOCK.

The fragments contained in this volume had been already collected, and were in course of preparation for the press, when my attention was called to an article ("Percy Bysshe Shelley. Supplementary Notice.") written by Mr. T. L. Peacock, in *Fraser's Magazine* for March of the present year. In this he offers some observations on a paper entitled "Shelley in Pall Mall," published by me in *Macmillan's Magazine* for June, 1860. I had said—

"Much has been written about Shelley during the last three or four years, and the store of materials for his biography has been augmented by many particulars—some authentic and valuable; others trivial, or mythical, or founded on mistakes or misrepresentations. It does not strictly fall within the scope of this paper to notice any of these, but some of the latter class are calculated to modify so injuriously what has hitherto been the prevalent estimate of Shelley's character; and, while entirely unfounded, are yet open to correction from the better knowledge of so few; that it would be inexcusable to omit an opportunity of comment which only chance has presented, and which may not speedily recur. It will be readily perceived that the allusion is to the statements respecting Shelley's separation from his first wife, published by Mr. T. L. Peacock in *Fraser's Magazine* for January last. According to these the transaction was not preceded by long-continued unhappiness, neither was it an amicable agreement effected in virtue of a mutual understanding. The time cannot be distant when these assertions must be refuted by the publication of documents hitherto withheld, and Shelley's family have doubted whether it be worth while to anticipate it. Pending their decision, I may be allowed to state that the evidence to which they would in such a case appeal, and to the nature of which I feel fully competent to speak, most decidedly contradicts the allegations of Mr. Peacock."

Mr. Peacock, however, persists in his opinion, and applies himself to "show, I will not say the extreme improbability, but the absolute impossibility of Shelley's family being in possession of any such documents as are here alleged to exist." His argument is chiefly based upon a comparison of dates. His article may still be procured at any circulating library, and I hope that all who are interested in Shelley will read it.

I am not about, on this occasion, to write the history of the connection of Shelley and his first wife,* nor to anticipate the interest of any forthcoming work by a premature publication of documents. It will be sufficient to observe that—

1. The papers referred to in *Macmillan's Magazine*, respecting the existence of which Mr. Peacock is so incredulous, demonstrate that Shelley and Harriet corresponded, both during the former's absence on the Continent and afterwards; that he visited her repeatedly after his return to England; that so late, at least, as December, 1814, he continued to take an affectionate interest in her, gave her much good advice, or what he regarded as such, and exposed himself to no little inconvenience and danger of misconstruction in a generous endeavour to promote her welfare; that previous to his departure from England he had given instructions that deeds should be prepared and a settlement executed for her benefit. The existence of documents to this effect is certain, for I have seen them.†
Whenever they are published, it will be acknowledged

---

* The origin of which, by the way, has been greatly obscured by the reference of certain important documents to a wrong date. The matter will be fully elucidated on another occasion.

† It should be stated that the most important of these documents has been discovered since the publication of Mr. Hogg's biography, but previous to the appearance of Mr. Peacock's first article (June, 1858).

that the above is a perfectly fair *resumé* of their contents, and the inference is too obvious to require to be pointed out.

2. So much for the terms on which Shelley and Harriet parted. A question of equal importance remains to be discussed. I had referred to the separation as " a transaction preceded by long-continued unhappiness." Mr. Peacock had said on the contrary (*Fraser's Magazine*, vol. lxi. p. 94), " There was no estrangement,* no shadow of a thought of separation, till Shelley became acquainted, not long after the second marriage [March 24, 1814], with the lady who was subsequently his second wife."

Now, in his anxiety to vindicate himself at Shelley's expense, Mr. Peacock has proved rather too much, and laboriously undermined the fabric of his own argument. He employs a considerable part of his supplementary paper in establishing, from an attentive scrutiny of the dates given in Mr. Hogg's biography, that " Shelley's

---

* Forgetting that he had said himself (vol. lvii., p. 654) : "I have often thought that if Harriet had nursed her own child, and if this sister had not lived with them, the link of their married love would not have been so easily broken. But of this hereafter, when we come to speak of the separation." When, however, he does come to speak of it, he does not say a word about Miss Westbrook. The two reasons here assigned are in reality but one. Harriet would undoubtedly have nursed her child if her sister had not lived with her ; the reason she did not was that the latter would not let her.

acquaintance with Miss Godwin must have begun between the 18th of April and the 8th of June; much nearer, I apprehend, to the latter than the former." Be it so. Then how could an acquaintance formed between April and June have occasioned an estrangement which, as we learn from Shelley himself, already existed in March? How comes it that Mr. Peacock, so lynx-eyed in eliciting from Mr. Hogg's volumes every little circumstance which he imagines may possibly be construed to Shelley's disadvantage, should have overlooked the most important original document they contain, a document utterly at variance with his view of the subject?

SHELLEY TO MR. HOGG.*

BRACKNELL, *March 16th*, 1814.

MY DEAR FRIEND,

I promised to write to you when I was in the humour. Our intercourse has been too much interrupted for my consolation. My spirits have not sufficed to induce the exertion of determining to write to you. My value, my affection for you have sustained no diminution; but I am a feeble, wavering, feverish being, who requires support and consolation, which his energies are too exhausted to return.

I have been staying with Mrs. B. for the last month;

* Hogg's Life of Shelley, vol. ii., pp. 513, 516.

I have escaped, in the society of all that philosophy and friendship combine, from the dismaying solitude of myself. They have revived in my heart the expiring flame of life. I have felt myself translated to a paradise, which has nothing of mortality but its transitoriness; my heart sickens at the view of that necessity, which will quickly divide me from the delightful tranquillity of this happy home—for it has become my home. The trees, the bridge, the minutest objects, have already a place in my affections.

My friend, you are happier than I. You have the pleasures as well as the pains of sensibility. I have sunk into a premature old age of exhaustion, which renders me dead to everything, but the unenviable capacity of indulging the vanity of hope, and a terrible susceptibility to objects of disgust and hatred.

My temporal concerns are slowly rectifying themselves; I am astonished at my own indifference to their event. I live here like the insect that sports in a transient sunbeam, which the next cloud shall obscure for ever.

I am much changed from what I was. I look with regret to our happy evenings at Oxford, and with wonder at the hopes which in the excess of my madness I there encouraged. Burns says, you know—

> "Pleasures are like poppies spread,
>   You seize the flower—the bloom is fled;
> Or like the snowfalls in the river,
>   A moment white—then lost for ever."

—— is still with us,—not here!—but will be with me when the infinite malice of Destiny forces me to depart. I am now but little inclined to contest this point. I certainly hate her with all my heart and soul. It is a sight that awakens an inexpressible sensation of disgust and horror, to see her caress my poor little Ianthe, in whom I may hereafter find the consolation of sympathy. . . . . . What have you written?—I have been unable even to write a common letter. I have forced myself to read Beccaria and Dumont's Bentham. I have sometimes forgotten that I am not an inmate of this delightful home,—that a time will come which will cast me again into the boundless ocean of abhorred society. I have written nothing but one stanza, which has no meaning, and that I have only written in thought:

> Thy dewy looks sink in my breast;
> Thy gentle words stir poison there;
> Thou hast disturbed the only rest
> That was the portion of despair;
> Subdued to Duty's hard control,
> I could have borne my wayward lot;
> The chains that bind this ruined soul
> Had cankered then, but crushed it not.

* * * * *

Believe me truly and affectionately yours,

P. B. SHELLEY.

Well may Mr. Hogg term this " a most touching, most

melancholy letter!" Is it the language of one happy in his domestic relations? or rather of one whose affections are blighted, whose hopes crushed, whose feelings fluctuate between agony and apathy, who "snatches a fearful joy" in the temporary refuge he has found from domestic infelicity, and trembles at the prospect of the time, so near at hand, when that, too, is to fail him? How touching, too, the plaintive resignation with which he postpones the hope of encountering sympathy in his own family, till his infant daughter shall be of an age to understand and return his affection! There can be but one answer to the question I have suggested; and if it be difficult to suppose Mr. Peacock unacquainted with the existence of this letter, it is impossible that he should have misconceived its purport, if he ever read it. Yet I had much rather adopt either of these alternatives, than the only one which remains—that he relied upon the ignorance of his readers. Let that pass, and let us be content with hoping that he will not again accuse Mary of having caused an estrangement which the dates adduced by himself prove to have existed before Shelley had seen her; and will acknowledge that whether Miss Westbrook were or were not "excusable"* in attributing the "ruin" of her sister to Shelley's acquaintance with his second wife, she could not be correct in so

* Expression attributed to Shelley in Miss Westbrook's affidavit. (*Fra. Mag.*, vol. lxv., p. 345.)

doing. It is hardly necessary to add what has been so frequently stated, that no conduct of Shelley's had any connection, direct or indirect, with Harriet's death.

The tone of the letter, moreover, implies that these domestic troubles were not of very recent origin, thus confirming Lady Shelley's mention of them as subsisting at the end of 1813. Mr. Peacock (vol. lxv., p. 344) has strangely misunderstood this passage. In speaking of them as having "come to a crisis," the editress of the "Shelley Memorials" merely meant that they had reached such a point as to render domestic felicity out of the question. In adding that "separation ensued," she by no means intended to be understood as stating that it ensued immediately; which assertion indeed, as Mr. Peacock himself points out, could not have been made by any one who had read Mr. Hogg's second volume.*

It is not my wish to bear hardly upon Mr. Peacock, but I cannot, in justice to my case, refrain from advert-

---

* As regards the state of Shelley's domestic affairs, so early as 1812, the evidence of his Welsh neighbour, Mrs. Williams, of Tanyrallt, is important and unequivocal. She says (in a letter addressed to a lady, a relative of the biographer of Leo X.): "He (Shelley) also met with other causes of sorrow to his kind, fine feelings. I fancy that his wife and her sister had neither of them much mind; they were not very suitable companions for such a man * * * It was not likely that peace and harmony would long reign in such elements; and he found confusion and anarchy in his house as well as poverty."

ing to a very marked instance of sophistry on his part. He says (vol. lxi., p. 92), "Captain Medwin represented this separation to have taken place by mutual consent; Mr. Leigh Hunt and Mr. Middleton adopted this statement." It is thus more ingeniously than ingenuously attempted to throw the responsibility of this version of the transaction upon Captain Medwin, a writer of little authority. Medwin's life of Shelley appeared in 1847; and I wish I could believe that Mr. Peacock did not know that the statement was made in Leigh Hunt's "Lord Byron and his Contemporaries," published in 1828 (p. 184). There is nothing relating to the manner of the separation in Medwin's "Conversations of Lord Byron" (1824); nor, if there had been, would it have followed that Leigh Hunt, who had access to first-hand sources of information, had derived his assertion from that book. It is worthy of remark, that Mr. Peacock's paper did not appear till after Leigh Hunt's death. What Leigh Hunt would have said to him may be inferred from the following paragraph from the *Examiner* of August 31st, 1817, written and printed while the Chancery suit was pending before Lord Eldon :—

A reporter in a morning paper (the *Chronicle*), after stating it to be "utterly impossible" that cases heard before the Chancellor can be in any degree "accurately reported," proceeds, nevertheless, to state what he considers to be the case of Westbrook *v.* Shelley, Esq. We are not about to enter into the particulars of the case ourselves, though we conceive that if statements that appear to tell for one side are allowed to transpire, the very greatest and most awful hints on the part of the noble and learned arbiter cannot reasonably act as a check to the publication of the others. But we happen to know a good deal of this remarkable and important question, as we shall hereafter show, if it is found necessary to bring it before the public; and we here notice it to correct two erroneous impressions to which the report in question might give rise, &c.

It thus appears that Shelley's friends were as ready to undertake the public vindication of his conduct in 1817 as in 1860. Why they did not do so we learn from Mr. Peacock himself, who says (vol. lxi., p. 101) that the Chancellor threatened to punish any report of the proceedings as a contempt of Court. This was hardly the behaviour of a magistrate conscious of his integrity.

3. This letter also proves that Shelley's formal re-marriage with Harriet is devoid of the importance which Mr. Peacock would attach to it. It took place on March 24th, eight days after the letter had been written, as if expressly to show that, whether or no the ceremony " could hardly have formed an incident in a series of long-continued unhappiness " (Mr. Peacock, vol. lxv., p. 343), it certainly *did* form such an incident. The fact of its having taken place could only surprise those unacquainted with the condition of Shelley's affairs at the time;* and the stress laid upon

* In a letter to his father, dated only eleven days previously, he says: " I lament to inform you that the posture of my affairs

it by Mr. Peacock suggests some doubts whether, after all, he is not himself one of the number. He does know, however, that it was of vital importance to Shelley's prospects that there should be no doubt as to the legitimacy of his heirs, while the very certificate he prints (vol. lxi., p. 94) states that " doubts have arisen concerning the validity of the said [Scotch] marriage." The fact speaks for itself; and it is not probable that Shelley or Harriet would have allowed their children's interests to suffer for want of a ceremony to which neither attached any but a legal significance. Similar motives induced Shelley to marry his second wife soon after the death of the first; though his subsequent writings unmistakeably indicate that his opinions on the subject of matrimony had undergone no alteration. The question, however, of Mr. Peacock's qualifications for pronouncing authoritatively upon Shelley's affairs, is one to which I shall find it necessary to recur.

4. Mr. Peacock says (vol. lxv., p. 344), " On the 7th of July, 1814, Harriet wrote to a mutual friend, still living, a letter, in which ' she expressed a confident belief that he must know where Shelley was, and entreating his assistance to induce him to return home.' *

is so critical that I can no longer delay to raise money by the sale of *post obit* bonds."

* I do not know whether these inverted commas are meant to indicate that Mr. Peacock has not seen the letter himself. If he has seen it, it is difficult to acquit him of wilful misrepresenta-

She was not even then aware that Shelley had finally left her." Mr. Peacock will probably be surprised to learn that not only are Shelley's representatives aware of the existence of this letter, but that it has long been in their possession, and that they contemplate its publication. Their surprise is that he should have so utterly misrepresented its contents. One phrase ("You are *his* friend, and you can feel for *me*") undoubtedly indicates the misunderstanding which, as we have already seen, had existed for at least six months. But Harriet does *not* "express a confident belief that her correspondent must know where Shelley is," or say or imply that she does not know herself. She does *not* entreat the correspondent's assistance to induce Shelley to return home, nor could she possibly have done so; for Mr. Peacock has concealed the all-important fact that the letter was written *from Bath to London*, and that, consequently, if Shelley had left his house at Bracknell, Harriet had left it also. His account of the letter is accordingly a felicitous combination of the *suppressio veri* and the *suggestio falsi*. Neither should we have learned from him that Harriet mentions having heard from Shelley only four days previously, and that the sole anxiety she betrays is for the latter's health.

tion. If he has not seen it, he should have stated the fact distinctly, and not left it to be conjectured by possibly inadvertent readers.

Finally, the letter was not, as Mr. Peacock states, *written* on July 7th, but *received* on that day. Now we know from unimpeachable MS. authority that the separation did not occur later than June 17; there is also the most conclusive evidence that Mary lived under her father's roof till July 28th; it is therefore untrue that Shelley forsook Harriet to elope with her. Nor was his departure from England the hasty and impulsive step usually represented; between June 17th and July 28th there was ample time for deliberation and the arrangement of perplexed family affairs. The circumstances immediately attendant upon this transaction have hitherto been greatly misunderstood. It has been described as "a flight;" and Harriet has been not unnaturally supposed to have been the person whose pursuit the fugitives were anxious to evade. But their MS. journal proves conclusively that they had no idea of any interference or opposition on her part. On the contrary, she was well acquainted with the fact of their journey, and expected to receive accounts of its progress. The person whose pursuit they apprehended was Mrs. Godwin, Mary's stepmother, who actually did follow them to Calais. Even her proceedings had no reference to Mary, but to the person (the C. of the letters and journals) who accompanied the travellers.

5. Much light has been recently thrown upon the feelings which actuated Shelley at this critical period of

his history, by an interesting and unexpected discovery made during the preparation of this volume. It appears that a poem, hitherto referred to the date of 1821, was in fact written in June, 1814, and addressed to Mary. The piece is as follows; —

TO ———.

Mine eyes were dim with tears unshed;
   Yes, I was firm—thus wert not thou;
My baffled looks did fear yet dread
   To meet thy looks—I could not know
How anxiously they sought to shine
With soothing pity upon mine.

To sit and curb the soul's mute rage
   Which preys upon itself alone;
To curse the life which is the cage
   Of fettered grief that dares not groan,
Hiding from many a careless eye
The scorned load of agony.

Whilst thou alone, then not regarded,
   The [—] thou alone should be,
To spend years thus, and be rewarded
   As thou, sweet love, requited me
When none were near—Oh! I did wake
From torture for that moment's sake.

> Upon my heart thy accents sweet
>   Of peace and pity fell like dew
> On flowers half dead ; thy lips did meet
>   Mine tremblingly ; thy dark eyes threw
> Their soft persuasion on my brain,
> Charming away its dream of pain.
>
> We are not happy, sweet! our state
>   Is strange and full of doubt and fear;
> More need of words that ills abate;—
>   Reserve or censure come not near
> Our sacred friendship, lest there be
> No solace left for thee and me.
>
> Gentle and good and mild thou art,
>   Nor can I live if thou appear
> Aught but thyself, or turn thine heart
>   Away from me, or stoop to wear
> The mask of scorn, although it be
> To hide the love thou feel'st for me.

This poem has hitherto been wholly unintelligible; no one could conjecture either the occasion of its composition or the person to whom it was addressed. The mystery is now elucidated, and the state of Shelley's feelings placed beyond dispute. While it is evident that he had conceived an ardent affection for Mary, and found his best refuge from his own domestic sorrows in her compassion,* it is equally manifest that, under a sense of obligation to another, he is doing his best to control the vehemence of his emotions. "A moment" of sympathy has consoled him for prolonged suffering, yet he dreads "censure" as much as "reserve," and deprecates imprudence no less than indifference. Something must have occurred to alter his views between the date of this poem and July 28th, and the amicable character of his subsequent relations with Harriet indicates this to have been the discovery that she, equally with himself, had ceased to expect happiness from a continuance of their connection. Two parted who never should have met; what is there in this that is not perfectly natural? And, notwithstanding certain insinuations which will require to be noticed more particularly, I do not mean to imply, and have never had the remotest idea of implying, that the circumstances attendant upon the separation were in any respect less creditable to Harriet than to Shelley.

6. We may now inquire a little into Mr. Peacock's

---

* Pending more explicit revelations, it may be hinted that circumstances existed to render Mary almost as much an object of sympathy to Shelley, as he himself was to her,—

> "And so they grew together like two flowers
> * * * which the same beams and showers
> Lull or awaken in their purple prime."

qualifications as a biographer of Shelley—always remembering that 1814 is not 1817, that Bracknell and London are not Marlow, and that no intimacy of subsequent acquaintance can render any person an authority with respect to events which occurred while that acquaintance was slight and occasional.

By his own account, his opportunities for the observation of Shelley's early married life were as follows:— " I saw Shelley for the first time in 1812, just before he went to Tanyrallt. I saw him again once or twice before I went to North Wales, in 1813. On my return he was residing at Bracknell, and invited me to visit him there. This I did." (Vol. lvii. p. 654.) Surely this does not amount to much, and, in fact, Mr. Peacock has done himself some injustice: he might have added that he accompanied the Shelleys on their second visit to Edinburgh; but, presumably for good reasons, he has chosen to keep this circumstance in the background. So much for his opportunities of observation; it remains to be examined whether he was the sort of person whom his acquaintances were likely to select as a confidant. Resisting all temptation to avail myself of any unpublished evidence that may have a bearing upon this question, I will content myself with adducing a letter which—not through the instrumentality of Shelley's family—has already found its way into print. Writing to Mr. Hogg, in October, 1813, Cornelia N.

thus refers to Mr. Peacock (Hogg, vol. ii., p. 477):
"They (the Shelleys) have made an addition to their party in the person of a cold scholar, who, I think, has neither taste nor feeling. This Shelley will perceive, sooner or later; for his warm nature craves sympathy, and I am convinced he will not meet it in his new acquaintance." There is no penetration like a woman's, and it would have been better for all parties had Shelley entirely concurred with his discerning friend. With his usual generosity,* however, he was disposed to view his new acquaintance in a somewhat more favourable light.

He thus writes to Mr. Hogg from Edinburgh †

---

* "He acted," says Mrs. Shelley (in Mr. Hogg's Preface, pp. 8 and 9), "from the fixed principle of endeavouring to benefit and improve each person with whom he had communion; and that mind must have been cold and depraved which did not experience this necessary result from his sensibility united to his urbanity." Such minds, however, must have existed, for curious illustrations could easily be given of the effects of Shelley's benevolent and, as it would appear, self-denying experiments. Before any one deliberately undertakes to annoy those who have treated him with signal kindness, he should consider whether his path of mischief may not happen to conduct him

"*per ignes
Suppositos cineri doloso.*"

† Respecting this second excursion to Edinburgh, Mr. Hogg observes, with great justice: "I marvelled at the rash and extravagant delusion, and was curious to learn by what evil

(vol. ii., p. 488) : "A new acquaintance is on a visit with us this winter. He is a very mild, agreeable man, and a good scholar. His enthusiasm is not very ardent, nor his views very comprehensive; but he is neither superstitious, ill-tempered, dogmatical, nor proud." It is immaterial to inquire whether Shelley's right hand had forgotten its cunning when it thus sketched the mild man with the negative character. Possibly the "cold scholar" might have proved warm enough had he been detected in a series of mistakes or misrepresentations. It is enough that this *was* Shelley's opinion of Mr. Peacock; and that, however amusing such a person might be as a companion, he was not one whom the poet would have thought of honouring or burdening with his confidence.* Of this fact Mr. Peacock himself has unintentionally afforded the most

---

counsellor it had been put into their (the Shelleys') heads. There was always a contest for him (Shelley) between forward, spunging vulgarity, that would live out of him, on the one hand; and on the other, the modest, fostering elegance that cherished him, and would have maintained him had it been needful." (Vol. ii., pp. 479, 480.)

* Shelley was much more chary of his confidence than might have been expected. Leigh Hunt informed Sir Percy and Lady Shelley that, although an inmate of Hunt's house when engrossed by the most painful family affairs, Shelley never once opened his lips upon the subject. *A fortiori* he was not likely to confide in Mr. Peacock—

"Hiding from many a careless eye,
The scornèd load of agony."

satisfactory evidence. He says (vol. lxv., p. 346): "Subsequently the feeling for Harriet's death grew into a deep and abiding sorrow, but it was not in the beginning that it was felt most strongly." He also states: "I never saw him (Shelley) more calm and self-possessed than a short time after this melancholy event." Therefore, with all Shelley's impulsiveness, he had more discretion than to make a confidant of Mr. Peacock. The proof consists in a series of letters, written by Shelley at this very time, to one in whom he did confide, and at present in the possession of his family. Nothing more beautiful or characteristic ever proceeded from his pen, and they afford the most unequivocal testimony of the grief and horror occasioned by the tragical incident to which they bear reference. Yet self-reproach formed no element of his sorrow, in the midst of which he could proudly say, " * * * * (mentioning two dry, unbiassed men of business) *every one* does me full justice, bears testimony to the uprightness and liberality of my conduct to her" (Harriet).

If deficiency of information be a disqualification for a biographer, an inaccurate recollection is something worse. Now, in almost the only instance where a statement of Mr. Peacock's is open to another test than that of its internal probability, it signally breaks down. He quotes (vol. lvi., p. 95) the following anecdote from Mr.

Hogg (vol. i., p. 423): "Shelley told me his friend Robert Southey once said to him, 'A man ought to be able to live with any woman: you see that I can,* and so ought you. It comes to pretty much the same thing I apprehend. There is no great choice or difference.'" Mr. Peacock perceives that this conversation is not very consistent with his assertions respecting the amity of Shelley and his wife, prior to the former's acquaintance with Mary Godwin. He, therefore, endeavours to show that it did not take place in 1811, but in 1814, *after the separation.* To corroborate this version of the incident, he tells the following story, for which he professes to have the authority of Shelley himself:—
"Shelley gave me some account of an interview he had had with Southey. It was after his return from his first visit to Switzerland, in the autumn of 1814. I forget whether it was in town or country; but it was in Southey's study, in which was suspended a portrait of Mary Wollstonecraft * * * Shelley had previously known Southey, and wished to renew or continue friendly relations; but Southey was repulsive. He pointed to the picture, and expressed his bitter regret that the daughter of that angelic woman should have been so misled. It was most probably on this occasion

---

* No one who has read Southey's correspondence can suppose that this remark was intended in disparagement of his wife. It was evidently merely jocular.

that he made the remark cited by Mr. Hogg." It is impossible that Shelley can have given Mr. Peacock "some account" of "an interview in the autumn of 1814," for it is impossible that such an interview can have taken place. It cannot have been in town, for Southey's study was at Keswick, and whatever his admiration for Mary Wollstonecraft, he did not carry her portrait about with him, and hang it up wherever he went.* It cannot have been at Keswick, for Shelley's diary, which accounts for every day of his life from July 28th, 1814, onwards, contains, besides many other matters hitherto unsuspected by Mr. Peacock, the clearest proof that after that period he never was thirty miles to the north of London. The conversation must consequently have taken place in 1811, long before Shelley's acquaintance with Mary Wollstonecraft's daughter, and the incident so circumstantially narrated by Mr. Peacock can have had no existence but in

---

* Since the above was written, I have been permitted to refer to a letter written by the Rev. Cuthbert Southey, shortly after the publication of Mr. Peacock's second article. Mr. Southey says: "Shelley passed some time at Keswick in the years 1811-12, and had then a good deal of intercourse with my father, who took much interest in him. After that time, they never met again. My father was not in London in 1814. He was there in the previous year, and for the first and last time met Lord Byron, but not Shelley." For Southey's own account of his acquaintance with Shelley, see his Correspondence, vol. iii., pp. 325, 326.

his own imagination. I will not say in the necessities of his argument, for I wish to compel him to acknowledge that it is perfectly possible to receive his statements respecting any particular conversation with great caution, without the impoliteness of casting any doubt upon his veracity.* He is, moreover, entitled to our especial indulgence, as his works consist principally of dialogues, in which, for the sake of raising a laugh, persons of celebrity are introduced under transparent disguises as giving utterance to sentiments which they certainly would not have recognised as their own. It is easily conceivable that the habit, thus engendered, of manufacturing conversations to suit a particular purpose, may be one which, with the best intentions, it is difficult to wholly lay aside.

Mr. Peacock will himself be the first to regret this unfortunate propensity when he perceives that it has betrayed him into injustice towards persons whom he cannot have intended to wound or injure. At vol. lxv. p. 345, we are favoured with a hint of another conversation, or rather series of conversations, held with unknown persons at unknown times and places, and to the following effect :—

* As he seems to apprehend may be the case (vol. lxv., p. 344)—*Non obtusa adeo gestamus pectora Pœni*—we would not for the world be guilty of so much rudeness. He appears to forget that he has just been impugning *my* veracity ; but, all things considered, I think I can afford to forgive him.

"Harriet suffered enough in her life to deserve that her memory should be respected. I have always said to all whom it might concern, that I would defend her to the best of my abilities, against all misrepresentations."

In plain English, statements injurious to Harriet's memory have appeared in the "Shelley Memorials," or some other authorised publication, and Mr. Peacock feels bound to come forward as her champion. I will allow that as the mediæval barons were wont to found expiatory chapels upon the scenes of their misdemeanors, so, after all the mischief which Mr. Peacock has occasioned by rash and groundless assertions, it might not be amiss if he were to undertake the defence of some one who actually did stand in need of skilful and not very scrupulous advocacy—himself, for example. But to his constituting himself Harriet's champion, there is one insuperable impediment. No one has attacked her. Nobody knows better than Mr. Peacock that there is not a syllable in the "Shelley Memorials," or any kindred work, reflecting upon Harriet in any way. I do not dispute that whosoever sits down to assail a deceased friend and benefactor is thereby placed in a disagreeable, an invidious, one might almost say an odious position. And I can well understand that it might be a great convenience to such a person if he could in any way contrive to create an impression that his behaviour was imposed upon him by the necessity of defending some one else. But Mr. Peacock's reputation, to say nothing of his self-complacency, forbids us to ascribe such motives to him for a moment. He will, therefore, hasten to offer a complete and graceful reparation, and relieve the pain of which it must grieve him to have been the involuntary cause.

To obviate further mistakes, I may as well state that Shelley's representatives will be as ready as Mr. Peacock himself to defend Harriet's character in the event of its encountering an assailant. The only manner in which they can conceive this contingency as likely to arise is by reason of its employment as a shield for Mr. Peacock. Let us hope that the precautions just adopted may prove effectual to avert so serious a misfortune.

I trust it will be apparent that I have no desire to bear hardly upon Mr. Peacock, but rather to interpret his proceedings *in meliorem partem.* That I have not always been able to do so may be the result of a deficiency in taste or sensibility. For example, I cannot profess to consider the picture, drawn with so much *naïveté* by himself, of a man spending twenty-one months* in a search for letters the effect of which he

---

* "I wrote the preceding note immediately after the appearance of Mr. Garnett's article (June, 1860), but I postponed its publication, in the hope of obtaining copies of the letters

expects will be to injure the memory of an old friend, as altogether of an edifying character. I certainly should not have liked to have been the painter or the exhibitor, much less the subject, of a sketch so eminently in the manner of Pyreicus.* As, however, Mr. Peacock has chosen to combine all three characters in his own person, it must be inferred that he views the matter in a different light. This is a question of taste; on subjects of greater personal interest to him I am happy to find that we are substantially agreed. I entirely concur with him (vol. lvii. p. 643) that a biographer " is bound to keep to himself whatever may injure the interests or hurt the feelings of the living, especially "—a judicious limitation—" when the latter have in no way injured or calumniated the dead." Whatever my feelings on commencing my task may have been, I do not, now that it is completed, consider that Mr. Peacock stands any longer in the position of one who has injured the dead, and I willingly concede to him the immunity he claims as the privilege of his innoxiousness.

Any reply that may be attempted to these observations will be amply considered upon the occasion to

which were laid before Lord Eldon in 1817" (Mr. Peacock, vol. lxv., p. 344). His article has just made its appearance (March, 1862).

* Smith's "Dictionary of Classical Biography," *s. v.*

which reference has already been made. The entire subject might have been, in some respects with advantage, postponed until that period, but it was felt that an omission of the present opportunity might be liable to misconstruction.

March 6, 1862.

LINES AT BOSCOMBE.

LINES AT BOSCOMBE.

So, Florence, you have shown to me
All your wild region by the sea;
The pines, mysterious to us both,
Distorted with a side-long growth
Of boughs irregularly spread,
And rough trunks ivy-garlanded;
The pathways indistinct and brief,
Littered with droppings of the leaf;
The bents' precarious and scant
Life on the mounds extravagant
Of sand towards the abysmal sea
Crumbling for ever silently;
The rain-worn gully; the embrown'd
Curve, sweeping half the horizon round,
Of low beach, smooth to the content
Of the caressing element;
The glad waves' unconstrained advance,
And simultaneous resonance,
And silvery flash; the roving skiff,
And Bournemouth's pier, and Studland's cliff,

Dulling its line of keenest white
In the warm prevalence of light;
And now we sit, you smile, I sigh,
What think we, Florence, you and I?

This vision to my fancy brought
Another Florence; I have thought
Of a remote, more azure sea,
Ship-bringer unto Italy;
Not where the sullied wave reflects
The smoke Vesuvius ejects,
Or ripplings wreathe their radiant smiles
Under Ligurian campaniles,
Or where the classic waters bring
Music around the ruining
Of the lost Baiae they inter
Blithely, or are the theatre
Where marvelling Messina sees
Morgana's airy witcheries:
But where forlorner floods have placed
Salt lips against the Pisan waste
Of sand the dry sirocco has
Heaped lavishly, and reeds and grass,
Fed by lagoons and swampy chains
Of ponds, where sole the heron reigns,
Till wroth and dissonant he goes,
Scared by the charging buffaloes;

Yet almost everywhere you see
The violet's blue fragility,
Nestling her little store of sweet
'Mid the stained sheddings at the feet
Of the old pine trees that appear
As universal there as here.

What is the subtle link between
The English and the Tuscan scene?
Not merely their accordant mood
Of independent solitude;
Not only that the eye might scan,
Ranging the realm Etrurian,
In pine, and knoll, and sand and sea,
Almost this region's mimicry;—
But that one Spirit doth efface
The differences of either place,
Making of each the same obscure
Ground of one radiant portraiture—
That Soul of planetary birth,
Tempered for some more prosperous Earth,
Happy, by error or by guile
Rapt from the star most volatile
That speeds with fleet and fieriest might
Next to the kernel of all light,
Fallen unwelcome, unaware,
On this low world of want and care,

Mistake, misfortune, and misdeed,
Passion and pang,—where not indeed
Ever might envious dæmon quell
The ardour indestructible;
The mood scarce human or divine,
Angelic half, half infantine;
The intense unearthly quivering
Of rapture or of suffering;
The lyre, now thrilling wild and high,
Now stately as the symphony
That times the solemn periods,
Comings and goings of the Gods,
And smitten with as free a hand
As if the plectrum were a wand
Gifted with magic to unbar
The silver gate of every star:—
And truly, Shelley, thine were strains
At once to fire and freeze the veins,
Such as were haply spells of dread
In the high regions forfeited,
Breathed less intelligibly for
The duller earthly auditor.

Yes, Shelley loved the forests dim
By Pisa's coast—here they love him!
Italian shades could only give
A refuge to the fugitive

Whom these retreats, where never came
His wandering foot, and with his name
Only fortuitously blent,
Own as their boast and ornament.
The woods, dark borderers of the wave
From Percy's shrine to Mary's grave,*
Whose sombre and perennial woof
Screens from the spray the cheerful roof
O'er high saloons and galleries spread
The relic-chambers of the dead!
There Florence, like a daisy's bloom
Fair on some old heroic tomb'
In modesty and ignorance,
The sweetness of your sunny glance
Descries, untutored to discern,
The secret of the silver urn
Shrining the ashes chill and grey
Of the rich heart that glowed alway,
The shredded locks—all trifles else
Whose worth Affection only tells,
With her still count, of all the most
The drops from the heart's innermost
Shed on the scrawled and blotted page
Which, when at last its spells engage

---

* *i.e.* From Christchurch, where Shelley's family have erected a splendid monument to his memory, to Bournemouth, where Mrs. Shelley is interred.

The free enthusiastic mood
And poetry of maidenhood—
Then shall not even this meaner chant
Be ineffectual ministrant
To wing the spirit, taught its strength,
With aspiration, till at length
Another look shall occupy
The brown arena of the eye
Fixed on me now with half distress
And wonder at my pensiveness.

1860.

APPENDIX.

APPENDIX.

The following most interesting letter, long mislaid, has come to light just as the last sheets of this volume are passing through the press: it consequently cannot be inserted in its proper place, but its importance entitles it to have an appendix to itself. There are accompanying papers which place the relations of Hunt and Byron in a clear light, and indicate in what sense the statement * of the former that the loan solicited from the latter by Shelley never reached him, is to be understood. The money arrived in England after his departure, and was doubtless employed by his friends in liquidating the liabilities he had incurred there. The obligation to Byron, however, was not the less on this account, and was freely acknowledged by Hunt; while Byron, on his part, took care to make it distinctly understood that the money was not intended as a gift, but as a loan, to be repaid out of the anticipated profits of the *Liberal*. When, therefore, Byron had virtually destroyed the *Liberal* by withdrawing the

* Page 107 of this book.

co-operation on the faith of which Hunt had quitted England, the latter felt justified in asking to be released from his indebtedness, with which request (though I have not at present access to MS. evidence on the subject) it cannot be doubted that Byron complied. The misunderstandings between the two were precisely of the nature that Shelley could most readily have appeased, or rather prevented altogether. "All that were now left of our Pisan circle established themselves at Albaro — Byron, Leigh Hunt, and Mrs. Shelley. I took up my quarters in the city of palaces. The fine spirit that had animated and held us together was gone! Left to our own devices, we degenerated apace." (Trelawny, "Recollections," p. 152.)

SHELLEY TO LEIGH HUNT.

PISA, *Jan.* 25, 1822.

MY DEAREST FRIEND,

I SEND you by return of post £150,—within 30 or 40 of what I had contrived to scrape together. How I am to assemble the constituents of such a sum again I do not at present see; but do not be disheartened,— we will all put our shoulders to the wheel. Let me not speak of my own disappointment, which, great as it is in not seeing you here, is all swallowed up in sympathy with your present situation. Our anxiety during the continuance of the succession of tempests which one morning seemed to rain lightnings into Pisa, and amongst others struck the palace adjoining Lord Byron's, and turned the Arno into a raging sea, was, as you may conceive, excessive, and our first relief was your letter from Ramsgate. Between the interval of that and your letter of December 28, we were in daily expectation of your arrival. Yesterday arrived that dated January 6.

Lord Byron had assigned you a portion of his palace, and Mary and I had occupied ourselves in furnishing it. Everything was already provided except bedding, which could have been got in a moment, and which we thought it possible you might bring with you. We had hired a woman cook of the country for you, who is still with us. Lord B. had kindly insisted upon paying the upholsterer's bill, with that sort of unsuspecting goodness which makes it infinitely difficult to ask him for more. Past circumstances * between Lord B. and me render it *impossible* that I should accept any supply from him for my own use, or that I should ask it for yours if the contribution could be supposed in any manner to relieve me, or to do what I could otherwise have done. It is true that I cannot, but how is he to be assured of this?

One thing strikes me as *possible*. I am at present

* These circumstances were *not* of a pecuniary nature.

writing the drama of "Charles the First," a play which, if completed according to my present idea, will hold a higher rank than the "Cenci" as a work of art. Would no bookseller give me £150 or £200 for the copyright of this play?* You know best how my writings sell, whether at all or not: after they failed of making the sort of impression on men that I expected, I have never until now thought it worth while to inquire. The question is now interesting to me, inasmuch as the reputation depending on their sale might induce a bookseller to give me such a sum for this play. Write to Allman, your bookseller, tell him what I tell you of "Charles the First," and do not delay a post. I have a parcel of little poems also, the "Witch of Atlas," and some translations of Homer's Hymns, the copyright of which I must sell. I offered the "Charles the First" to Ollier, and you had better write at the same time to learn his terms. Of course you will not delay a post in this.

The evils of your remaining in England are inconceivably great if you ultimately determine upon Italy; and in the latter case, the best thing you can do is, without waiting for the spring, to set sail with the very first ship you can. Debts, responsibilities, and expenses will enmesh you round about if you delay, and force you back into that circle from which I made a

* See page 107 of this volume.

push to draw you. The winter, generally, is not a bad time for sailing, but only that period which you selected, and another when the year approaches to the vernal equinox. You avoided—and if you must still delay, will still avoid—the halcyon days of the Mediterranean. There is no serious danger in a cargo of gunpowder, hundreds of ships navigate these electrical seas with that freight without risk. Marianne would have been benefited, and would still benefit exceedingly, by the Elysian temperature of the Mediterranean.

Poor Marianne! how much I feel for her, and with what anxiety I expect your news of her health! Were it not for the cursed necessity of finding money, all considerations would be swallowed up in the thought of her; and I should be delighted to think that she had obtained this interval of repose which now perplexes and annoys me. * * * * *

Pray tell me in answer to this letter, unless you answer it in person, what arrangement you have made about the receipt of a regular income from the profits of the *Examiner*. You ought not to leave England without having the assurance of an independence in this particular; as many difficulties have presented themselves to the plan imagined by Lord Byron, which I depend upon you for getting rid of.* And if there is

---

* "When he [Byron] consented to join Leigh Hunt and others in writing for the *Liberal*, I think his principal inducement

time to write before you set off, pray tell me if Ollier has published "Hellas," and what effect was produced by "Adonais." My faculties are shaken to atoms, and torpid. I can write nothing; and if "Adonais" had no success, and excited no interest, what incentive can I have to write? As to reviews, don't give Gifford, or his associate Hazlitt, a stripe the more for my sake.* The man must be enviably happy whom reviews can make miserable. I have neither curiosity, interest, pain, nor pleasure in anything, good or evil, they can say of me. I feel only a slight disgust, and a sort of wonder that they presume to write my name. Send me your satire when it is printed. I began once a satire upon satire, which I meant to be very severe; it was full of *small knives*, in the use of which practice would have soon made me very expert.

was the belief that John and Leigh Hunt were proprietors of the *Examiner;* so when Leigh Hunt, at Pisa, told him he was no longer connected with that paper, Byron was taken aback, finding that Hunt would be entirely dependent upon the success of their hazardous project, while he would himself be deprived of that on which he had set his heart—the use of a weekly paper in great circulation." (Trelawny, "Recollections," p. 155.) It must be remembered, however, that the *Liberal* was a project of Byron's own—see Shelley's letter of Aug. 26.

* The juxtaposition of these names appears singular; but see Hunt's letters of July 10 and August 28, 1821, in the correspondence published by his son.

[*Postscript by Mrs. Shelley.*]

Dearest Children,

I fill up a little empty space of blank paper with many wishes, regrets, and &cs. Stay no longer, I beseech you, in your cloud-environed isle, as cloudy for the soul as for the rest of it. Even friends there are only to be seen through a murky mist, which will not be under the bright sky of dear Italy. My poor Marianne will get well, and you all be light-hearted and happy. Come quickly.

Affectionately yours,

MARY S.

THE END.

SHELLEYANA PUBLISHED BY MESSRS. MOXON & CO.

I.

SHELLEY MEMORIALS,

FROM AUTHENTIC SOURCES.

EDITED BY LADY SHELLEY.

Second Edition, price 5s.

Also,

II.

RECOLLECTIONS OF THE LAST DAYS OF SHELLEY AND BYRON.

BY E. J. TRELAWNY.

Post 8vo, price 9s.

III.

THE LIFE OF PERCY BYSSHE SHELLEY.

BY THOMAS JEFFERSON HOGG.

Vols. I. and II., price 21s.

BY THE EDITOR OF THIS VOLUME.

IO IN EGYPT, AND OTHER POEMS.

BY RICHARD GARNETT.

Price 5s.

BELL AND DALDY, 186, FLEET STREET.

POEMS FROM THE GERMAN.

BY RICHARD GARNETT.

Price 3s. 6d.

BELL AND DALDY, 186, FLEET STREET.